RUN

LIKE A CHAMPION

RUN
LIKE A CHAMPION

——

AN OLYMPIAN'S APPROACH
FOR EVERY RUNNER

ALAN CULPEPPER
with BRIAN METZLER

Boulder, Colorado

 **velopress®**

3002 Sterling Circle, Suite 100
Boulder, Colorado 80301-2338 USA
(303) 440-0601 · Fax (303) 444-6788
E-mail velopress@competitorgroup.com

Distributed in the United States and Canada by Ingram Publisher Services

A Cataloging-in-Publication record for this book is available from the
Library of Congress.
ISBN 978-1-937715-07-6

For information on purchasing VeloPress books,
please call (800) 811-4210, ext. 2138, or visit www.velopress.com.

This paper meets the requirements of ANSI/NISO Z39.48-1992
(Permanence of Paper).

Cover design by Moxie Sozo and Andy Omel
Interior design by Lora Lamm
Author photo by Brad Kaminski

Text set in Sentinel

15   16   17/10   9   8   7   6   5   4   3   2   1

SPECIAL THANKS TO

My wife, Shayne, and our four boys

My parents and my two brothers, Doug and Chris

Sam Walker and Mark Wetmore

CONTENTS

FOREWORD

Alan Culpepper should go down as one of the great American distance runners, both during the era in which he competed—from the mid-1990s to 2008—but also compared to the country's all-time greats. I have always had a deep respect for Alan because he trained so hard, competed so hard, yet always seemed to have the right balance between running and family—and that says a lot about who he is. He was a fierce competitor with a lot of talent, but he was also very humble and understated in his approach. The key to his success, as you will see in the pages of this book, is that he persistently followed a set of underlying principles that are universal to the development of distance runners of all ages and abilities. He trained hard, but he trained smartly and consistently with the continued application of these principles and a strict attention to detail.

Although he won many races and competed with the world's best runners in the world's biggest races, perhaps the biggest achievement of his career was his consistency. For almost 10 years, he never failed to finish among the top three of a U.S. championship race when an Olympic or world championship team berth was on the line. That's hard to do in the sport of distance running because you've got to be at your best at one specific moment on one specific day. Everything has to be just right—you have to be healthy, you have to be fit, you have to be peaking at the right time—yet you also have to be mentally focused and ready to compete as hard as you ever have. For Alan to do that and make two Olympic teams and four world championship teams over a 10-year period is phenomenal. It's a sign that he worked extremely hard, was very disciplined, and did the small things on a regular basis. It also shows that he was a true competitor of the highest order, both physically and mentally.

Alan and I duked it out for a long time over the course of our careers. I remember when he won the 1996 NCAA 5,000-meter run during his final year at the University of Colorado (CU) and how impressed I was. (I was a sophomore at UCLA and finished a distant ninth place in that race, 26 seconds behind Alan.) I continued to follow him after he turned pro, and after I finished college and turned pro, I found myself racing against him several times a year, from national championships to major international races. We were always friendly and polite with each other, but we were rivals too. Alan is a great guy, a very gracious competitor, but he was one of the toughest competitors out there. We always shook hands before and after the race, but during the race it was always "May the best man win." He got his fair share, and I got my fair share. When you were in a race with Alan, you knew it was going to be a fight to the finish. I know he made me better than who I was, and I hope I made him better than who he was.

Our careers started to take off at about the same time. We had gone head-to-head at the 2000 U.S. Olympic Trials in the 10,000-meter run in Sacramento, California, with me narrowly edging him by three-hundredths of a second to win in 28:03:32 as we earned our first Olympic team berths. In the next few years, we both moved up to the marathon in anticipation of the 2004 Olympics. Alan had run 2:09:41 in his debut at the 2002 Chicago Marathon, and I had run 2:12:35 at the 2002 New York City Marathon and 2:10:03 at the 2003 Chicago Marathon.

Heading into the 2004 U.S. Olympic Trials Marathon in Birmingham, Alabama, Alan was the favorite to win. But when the race started,

Brian Sell went out hard, hammering away out front to try to make the Olympic team. Instead of reacting and trying to chase him down, a few of us trusted our training and our instincts and did the work to reel him in. We finally caught Brian around mile 21, and that was where the real race began among Alan, Dan Browne, and me. It was a three-man race with about 5 kilometers to go, but it came down to just me and Alan over the final 2 miles. Alan had better closing speed than I did, so I knew if I had any chance of winning, I had to make a move right there.

With a little less than 400 meters to go, I tried to make a move. I started to wind up my speed and could feel my legs respond with a quicker cadence and a more powerful style for a few strides. But that only got Alan going too, and he just blew me away down the final stretch. He finished in 2:11:42, and although I wasn't far behind in 2:11:47, it was a true testament to Alan's fierce competitiveness, consistent training, and tactical racing abilities. He won the race decisively that day and earned his second Olympic berth. I was both thrilled that he had won and excited that I had made my second Olympic team too. There was never a grudge about that or even a wish on my part that I had won the race. It was one of those things where we all raced well and put it out there, and to finish second behind Alan after such a great race was very exciting for me.

The best thing the Olympic Trials race—and losing to Alan—did for me was that it helped motivate me in the months that followed. Based on the effort that Alan and I and Dan gave at that race, and knowing the competition would be that much greater in Athens, I trained harder than ever before. It was inspiring knowing we would be running in Greece, where the marathon had its origins. Before the Olympics, the U.S. marathon team spent the final days together on the island of Crete, and I knew from our shake-out runs that Alan and I were both very fit and ready to go. Even though we were both preparing to be as competitive as possible in the race of our lives, we were teammates and talked about strategies such as helping each other spot aid stations as we approached them.

In the end, we both ran very well that day. My silver medal and Deena Kastor's bronze medal in the women's marathon might have overshadowed Alan's effort, but Alan ran a very strong race in Athens too. He finished 12th in hard conditions that ultimately forced 20 runners to drop from the race. If you consider that four years earlier in Sydney, the United States had had only one entry in the Olympic marathon because there weren't many American runners fast enough to make the Olympic standard, to have Alan and me both finish in the top 12 in Athens was a big deal and probably one of the key moments in the revival of distance running in the United States.

One of my most memorable moments in Athens was right after the race. As soon as we saw each other after the finish, I remember Alan giving me an enormous bear hug. In that hug, I could sense how genuinely happy he was for me, and yet it was a celebration for each of us and a reflection of the efforts we had put into training and into that day. It was also a sign of the respect we had—and continue to have—for each other. Alan is a true competitor and a true gentleman.

MEB KEFLEZIGHI
2004 OLYMPIC MARATHON, SILVER MEDAL
2009 NEW YORK CITY MARATHON CHAMPION
2014 BOSTON MARATHON CHAMPION

INTRODUCTION

AN OLYMPIAN'S APPROACH TO RUNNING

It's 2 p.m. on Friday, July 14, 2000. In about six hours, I will be running the final of the 10,000-meter run at the U.S. Olympic Trials in Sacramento, California. I am staying in a DoubleTree hotel, not much different from all the other hotels I have stayed in at other races in the early years of my professional running career, but this time it feels much, much different. Not the hotel itself but the unfamiliar overpowering press of emotion and anxiety that feels a little like suffocating as I sit on the bed and wait for what is coming in a few hours' time. I am 27 years old and have competed in hundreds of races since I was a kid, but nothing of this magnitude. I competed in the 5,000-meter run at the 1996 U.S. Olympic Trials in Atlanta, but the pressure wasn't there because I was fresh out of college and didn't think I had any chance to finish in the top three and make the U.S. team. Perhaps back then I was young and naive, or maybe exhausted from a long college season that had concluded with my winning the National Collegiate Athletic Association (NCAA) title in the 5,000 meters. Whatever it was, it was different from what I am experiencing in Sacramento. This time the feeling is of being in the midst of something surreal, like a dream. And in a very real sense, it is a dream, realized. When I was 15, I wrote on a piece of spiral-notebook paper that I wanted to make the U.S. Olympic team in track and field. The goal I set for myself some 12 years ago is, today, right in front of me.

The U.S. Olympic Trials are without question the most intense and stressful event I have ever been a part of as a runner. You have prepared for four long years for a single day, a single race, where everyone on the start line has the single common goal of finishing among the top three. There are typically five or six athletes in every middle-distance and long-distance race who have a legitimate shot at making the team, based on their previous experience, and there are also a few wild cards whom no one expects to make the Olympic team who wind up running really well under pressure. But the difference between running well and making the Olympic team can be light-years apart. Making an Olympic team doesn't happen by accident or fluke but instead is a function of several factors. First you have to qualify for the trials by hitting a USA Track and Field (USATF) time standard. Next you have to finish in the top three in your race on that given day. Finally, if you haven't already, you need to hit an Olympic-qualifying time standard dictated by the International Association of Athletic Federations (IAAF). This time standard is much quicker than the USATF qualifying time to reach the trials—so in theory, you could finish in the top three in your race but not earn a spot on the U.S. Olympic team.

In 1996, I had taken a significant step toward my dream by qualifying for the Olympic Trials. When I qualified that year, I was fresh off a thrilling win of the NCAA 5,000 title in Eugene, Oregon. No one aside from my then girlfriend and now wife knew that I was battling a chest cold that day that had me coughing during the race, trying desperately to release the junk building in my lungs. With 500 meters to go, I bolted to the front, having hung off the pace for the entire race. After taking the lead, I held on to win with a 56-second last lap in the final race of my college career.

I came into the 1996 trials not favored to make the team and not fully grasping what it meant to compete at that level. This was the first race I had ever competed in where I was so thickly surrounded by professionals of the sport. Those guys were my idols—guys I had followed, read about, and watched for years. Guys like Pat Porter, who was nearing the end of an incredible career and whose pictures from *Track & Field News* I had pinned to my wall during high school. And Bob Kennedy, the favorite that day, was the American record holder in the event and on the verge of becoming the first U.S. runner to ever break the 13-minute barrier for the 5,000. (At the time, my best time in the 5,000 was the 13:31 I had recorded at the Mt. Sac Relays a few months earlier.)

At those 1996 trials, I ran in a way that left no doubt that I was ready for the next step, showing a level of confidence and nerve that surprised even me. I won my preliminary race, which qualified me for the final, and then, two days later, I led for several laps of the final. Neither tactic is advisable, especially for a young, inexperienced runner, and they exposed my immaturity. I wound up a distant 10th of 16 runners in the final, but I left Atlanta encouraged. I had proved that I was not afraid to be there, to run in the front, to compete against the nation's best, and to put myself in a position to win.

During the next three years, I continued to improve on that performance and showed that I was ready and capable of making the next step. In 1997, just a year after finishing 10th at the 1996 Olympic Trials, I finished as the runner-up in the 5,000 at the U.S. Track and Field Championships and earned my first chance to represent the United States in the World Championships in Athens, Greece. In 1999, I won national titles in both cross country and the 10,000 on the track, and I advanced to the World Championships in each one. By 2000, I was in a different position altogether than I had been in 1996 going into the U.S. Olympic Trials. I was no longer an unknown quantity or an inexperienced runner; this time I was heavily favored to make the team, and that changed every aspect of the experience. Instead of going into the race with no expectations (as in 1996), this time there were huge expectations. I was an established runner with a pro contract, and it was imperative that I make the team. But I knew that a lot of very good American runners had gone their entire careers without making it to the Olympics and that there was no such thing as a sure thing or any guarantee of a second chance later in my career. As far as I was concerned, this was it.

———

I sit on the bed in my room at the DoubleTree, trying to calm my mind and stomach. I tell myself I have prepared for 15 years for this moment, that I am healthy, that my training has gone well, that I am ready, and that I have no excuse not to run well.

———

The truth is, sometimes having no excuses is tougher than having to make one; after all, excuses come in handy—a minor injury, a sore throat, or something as mundane as a pair of socks that rub and cause irritation. It is not uncommon for runners to have something come up right before a significant race. Not something that keeps them from competing but rather something small that lets them off the hook emotionally by giving them a mental out. It is a kind of coping mechanism to help you handle the disappointment in case the thing you really want doesn't go the way you want it to. It's human nature, and we've all done it, but such escape hatches won't further your cause or get you to your goal. The greatest athletes I have known or read about don't give in to excuses, whether real or imagined. Rather, they want everything in their preparation to have gone well, with no issues or variables distracting their focus.

―――――――

The years, the experiences, the physical preparation, the sacrifices, the details, the thinking, thinking, thinking about this moment—and now it is about to happen. My day to this point has gone the way race day typically does: sleeping in as best I could (which is always hard to do because as soon as you are even remotely awake, you realize where you are and remember what is coming); a short jog followed by my usual stretching routine; rehydration and eating my one significant meal of the day; then lying around the hotel for hours, trying to relax. Now it's 2 p.m., and I am sitting on the bed. As the credits begin to roll on a movie I have just finished watching, I start to fully recognize the enormity of this moment. I barely paid attention to that movie—it was just something to kill time. It wasn't the movie that led to a rush of emotions but simply the combination of the music playing at the end of it and my feeling utterly overwhelmed. I cannot hold in my emotions anymore; they have to come out, and do they ever. Twenty-seven years old, alone and sobbing in my hotel room. This is the first time I have ever been so emotional before a race. Always nervous, yes, and fully aware of how emotional racing can be, but never at this level. I am suddenly flooded with fears: scared of what is in front of me, scared that I won't run to my potential, scared that I am going to return to this DoubleTree disappointed with the outcome. I say a prayer asking for strength, for courage, and not necessarily for the win but rather to simply run knowing I did my best.

―――――――

I've struggled and made my share of mistakes along the way, but the ace up my sleeve is that I've always handled the pressure to perform well. Even as a teen, just starting out and on the cusp of grasping how good I could be, I was able to run my best when it counted. This ability to handle intense situations is, along with the physical attributes, part of a person's given talent package. However, just like physical trainability, mental skills can be honed. I received excellent instruction in this when I was introduced to the sport of running and continued learning it throughout my impressionable college years. My first coach, Sam Walker, gave me a solid foundation on which to build, both physically and mentally, and Coach Mark Wetmore encouraged my progression at the University of Colorado. I remember being in high school, running inside the University of Texas Stadium in Austin at the state meet. I was 16 years old. There were 25,000 parents, coaches, athletes, family members, and other fans in the stands, a massive stage for a young man, and I was able to rise to the occasion and compete at my best. I was in a similar situation as a college senior at the NCAA meet in Eugene. The crowds in Eugene are famous for their enthusiasm, knowledge, and excitement during a race. Being there was even more incredible than I had imagined, but again, I was able to manage my emotions and perform my best that day. I might be as proud of that as I am of the podium finish.

———

By the time I get to the track later that evening, my nerves have settled. Being at the track, even though there are thousands of fans and a lot of commotion, is much better than being alone in a hotel room. I go through my typical warm-up routine—which is hardly necessary because it is pretty warm—and get ready to race. There are still some butterflies leading up to the start of the race, but my confidence is increasing by the minute. I trust my training, feel good, and am ready to do what I have come to do.

When the race gets under way, Abdi Abdirahman is one of several athletes to set a solid pace, along with Meb Keflezighi, Brad Hauser, and Jim Jurcevich. I mix it up in the early going too as we come through the 5,000-meter halfway mark in 14:11, but it is Keflezighi sitting behind Abdirahman out in front. With eight laps to go (roughly 2 miles), Keflezighi surges a bit with a couple of fast laps that give him a bit of a lead. I know I have to be aggressive and stay in contact if I want to finish in the top three, but I don't want to be too aggressive. With five laps to go, I push past Abdirahman with Brad Hauser on my heels and find myself about 50 meters behind Keflezighi. After shaking Hauser, I continue to gain ground on Keflezighi, but I'm still quite a ways back with a lap to go. That's when I summon every ounce of energy I can muster and unleash a massive finishing kick in pursuit of victory. Between the time I left the hotel and the start of the final lap of the race, the wavering emotion and nervousness I was experiencing have been replaced by a sharply focused understanding of how I can grasp the opportunity in front of me. And in that moment, the fatigue and strain of my body seem to melt away as a feeling of complete exhilaration overtakes my mind and body. It's as if I'm running on air, barely touching the ground with my spikes. As I come off the final turn to the homestretch, Keflezighi is sprinting too. I have enormous momentum and know he is within reach. The mad dash to the finish line is a culmination of all of my hard work and preparation over the previous four years. I am flying down the track, and so is Keflezighi. It is going to be a photo finish!

In the end, I run out of real estate, and Keflezighi nips me by less than one-tenth of a second. It is the slimmest of margins for a 25-lap race that took 28 minutes to complete. But, as much as I would love to have won that race, I am OK with how it worked out. Even though I didn't win, there is no question that I ran one of the best races of my life against some of the best runners in the country. I gave my all, competed to the very end, and achieved my goal of making the U.S. Olympic team that will be headed to

Sydney, Australia, in two months for the Games of the XXVIIth Olympiad. After years of training, learning, growing, progressing, and never relenting in what I believed, I have fulfilled a lifelong dream and become an Olympian.

——————

Isn't that what we all want out of our pursuits in this sport? To run to our potential? To run in such a way that we know we gave our best effort? To run knowing that we could not have run any better on the day when it counted? To not return to the DoubleTree disappointed with the results? Whether you are trying to qualify for a regional meet in high school cross country, qualify for the Boston Marathon, beat your personal best in your next half-marathon, or break 3 or 4 hours in a marathon for the first time, as committed runners we all have the same desire to meet our potential, to feel that we gave our best on that day. The feelings are the same no matter what your level, background, or current personal record (PR). Sure, the intensity and pressure to perform are heightened when trying to make an Olympic team or when running is your livelihood, but ultimately we all want the same result.

Great performances and the ability to perform when it matters most to you or when the stakes are high do not happen by accident. My club coach, Sam, always said, "Be ready when it counts," and interestingly enough, Mark Wetmore reiterated the same phrase in my college years. That phrase not only has stuck with me but has been the central focus of my entire career.

I have been fortunate to have been able to pursue running as a career, and one of the aspects I am most proud of during my time as a pro is my consistency across those years. I managed to stay at the top of the U.S. ranks for almost 10 years without any lapses or years where I just did not run well or did not perform well at the nationals. I finished in the top three in the U.S. National Championships in the 5,000,

10,000, marathon, and/or cross country from 1997 through 2007, and as a result, I never missed an opportunity to earn a spot on an Olympic or world championships team in the event I was focusing on. That consistency is one of the things in my career that I'm most proud of—mostly because I know consistent performance across time isn't something I lucked into or that happened because I was the most genetically gifted. Rather, I achieved that consistency because I understood that being ready when it counts is a function of aspects outside an athlete's training regimen. Being able to perform well year after year is more than just executing long runs, tempo runs, speed work, and hill repeats. In order to reach your full potential, you have to think beyond the training and envision a more comprehensive approach.

There have been countless discussions in training books—many full of great insight and knowledge—on what is required to perform at a particular level. This book is not a training book in that sense. Rather, it is meant to be a guide or a template of how to formulate a consistently winning approach, whatever your ability level. Most of the greatest distance runners of our time have adopted these principles whether they realized it or not. I say *most* great distance runners because some have unfortunately fallen short of their potential, in large part because they failed to recognize the often underscrutinized areas that needed improving—not necessarily training adaptations but other aspects we will discuss in this book. There are also those few supremely talented runners who are great despite themselves, but inevitably, and almost without exception, their careers are cut short by a lack of proper balance.

I have learned some very important lessons from these and other high-level runners with whom I shared the stage over the years, some of whose stories I will share in the chapters that follow. Those who came before me, and my own experiences, have taught me much, and this for sure: There are no secret training programs, no gimmicks, no magical workouts or catchy mantras that will alone take you to your best performance. I wish it were that simple. Most of us are ready and very willing to work hard and unafraid to do what it takes. But the reality is that consistent, great performance comes out of more than simply training. A holistic methodology must be adopted. It requires an all-encompassing viewpoint, not an all-consuming but a comprehensive thought process that helps you, the athlete and the person, fully develop your potential. Limiting your mind-set to just the training will inevitably limit your performance. Of course the training is extremely important, and I will go into a detailed explanation of the key components and, as importantly, the timing of those components. The reality, however, is that we are complex creatures with complex minds and lives. We should not limit our approach to strictly the physiological because that gets at only a portion of the far bigger, far more wonderful and complex picture of who we are and who we can be as athletes.

Let me be very clear that the insights shared in this book come from my personal experiences and those of other athletes whom I competed against or whom I know well. I have been fortunate to be professionally involved with the sport of running for 25 years. I started as a young boy, and there have been no periods since that time when running has not played a major part in my life. I consider myself to be highly perceptive, not only when it comes to internal reflection but also with other athletes whom I have admired as idols or competed against as rivals. I have also coached numerous recreational runners and discovered common themes worth reflecting on. I am not a sports psychologist, not a doctor, not a physical therapist, chiropractor, or physiologist. My expertise is based on applied science: living and feeling what I will share in the coming chapters. I have a very good comprehensive understanding of all the areas we will cover but do not presume to be an expert on any area.

At the end of the day, my objective is simple: to help others be successful, to help them feel the profound satisfaction that comes from accomplishing a difficult goal. I want to meet you right where you are and come alongside your efforts, perhaps expose a few areas that need improving, which will allow you to continue your progression and achieve personal satisfaction and greatness in your performance.

In 2007, I won U.S. national cross country championships at age 34, at a time in my career when it is safe to say I was considered beyond my prime. That race stands out personally as a highlight of my career. I ran like a true veteran, a professional, with patience and confidence. There were several younger American standouts in that race, and, in fact, three different runners led that race in the early going. But I prevailed by trusting my training, running my own race, and following my well-honed instincts. My effort was the culmination of all the aspects that I will share in this book, an application of the various elements that are required in order to run to your potential no matter how long you have been running or how fast you have been to this point. Whether you are brand-new to running or well beyond your supposed prime, young or old, the principles are the same. This road map should unlock areas of weakness in your overall preparation and expose aspects you might not have considered. My hope and goal here are to equip you to truly go after your own goals and fulfill your potential to run like a champion.

-1-

TRAINING WITH INTENTION

If I asked you what kind of runner you want to be, what would you say? Do you know? Can you describe your intentions in a sentence? Do you have a specific idea tied to a particular goal? Your first step in determining where you will go with your running and what you will accomplish is to figure out what kind of runner you really want to be.

It's a seemingly simple question, but settling on a precise answer takes some thinking and some context. One of my primary objectives in this book is to help runners realize their goals, something I aim to do with a several-pronged strategy: giving you the tools for a sound mental approach to running, showing you how to create balance in your life as it relates to running, helping you maximize your training, and developing your instincts to improve your racing. But to do any of that—before you even lace up your running shoes—you have to know what kind of runner you want to be and then commit to doing what it takes to get there.

It starts with examining your motivation for running. Your goals might be tied to a time or a race or a more abstract concept. Are you running to lose weight? To stay active as you get older? To check off a bucket-list race or set a new PR? Or simply to continue to grow and progress in your running throughout your life? Defining your motivation to run will help you to figure out what type of training you'll do. If your goal, for example, is to finish a big-city marathon like those in New York, Chicago, Houston, or Los Angeles, then your plan of attack will differ from that of one who is trying to break a 1:30 half-marathon or qualify for the Boston Marathon.

Being clear about your motivation will help you figure out what kind of runner you need to be to make your goals a reality. Then you'll have not only a more effective training experience but a more enjoyable one as you train with intention, using the correct program and appropriate intensity.

Finding Your Inspiration

During the original running boom between the early 1970s and the mid-1980s, many new runners were inspired by the elite athletes whom they saw racing on TV, competing in local races, and featured in magazines. Frank Shorter's victory in the 1972 Olympic marathon in Munich set off the spark among Americans, and his silver-medal performance four years later in Montreal continued to fan the fire and help build a new category of recreational, or enthusiast, runners. Then Bill Rodgers became an American icon for winning the Boston Marathon and New York City Marathon four times apiece between 1976 and 1980. As running gained mainstream appeal, more and more people were hitting the pavement, training to run fast in races from the 10K to the marathon, inspired by Shorter, Rodgers, and a few other runners who had become household names. At the same time, "jogging," a much less intense style of running, was also gaining appeal, allowing less-competitive or less-athletically-inclined people to run for fitness rather than fast race finishes.

Joan Benoit Samuelson's win in the 1984
Olympic marathon in Los Angeles was another
big moment in the original running boom and
a key catalyst in the explosion of the women's
running movement. While there were many
women running pioneers before Samuelson,
her win came at a time when American society was changing and
women were just starting to become empowered to chase their fitness goals. Benoit Samuelson was pure, unadulterated inspiration
for legions of new runners.

It starts with examining your motivation for running.

But it would be simple and shortsighted to think that hundreds of
thousands of people started running back then just because of a handful
of inspiring performances from a few iconic runners. Certainly those
were seminal moments in the growth of running, and Shorter, Rodgers, Samuelson, and others played a decisive role. But the real reason
running boomed, and continues to grow today, is because of what it
meant—on a very personal level—to runners then and still means to
runners now. Large-scale events with 20,000 bibbed racers and weekly
social-group runs aside, in the end, running is largely an individual
pursuit, and it's all about what it means to you. What do you get out
of running? What inspires you to run? Thoughtful answers to those
questions will help you determine what kind of runner you want to be.

At one level, running is one of the most basic and pure sports. It
involves simple human movement from one place to another. Because
running can be so simple—all you need are running shoes, a pair of
shorts, and a T-shirt—it is accessible to more people than any other
sport or recreational fitness activity.

But it's not just ease and accessibility that compel people to run. A
lot of activities are easy and accessible—swimming, bicycling, bowling, and jumping rope, for example. It is what running makes us feel
and allows us to accomplish that truly set it apart from other sports,

activities, and pastimes. Ask any lifelong runner: Running on a consistent basis—with or without a goal tied to a race—is addictive, but it may be the healthiest addiction you will ever have. It is a sure avenue to improving and maintaining fitness, creating a healthier lifestyle, finding peace of mind, even possibly lowering your risk of illness and disease. Just a few weeks into training, any new runner can feel the positive physiological, mental, and emotional changes running can bring about. Those are the primary reasons that so many people become passionate lifelong runners.

Those benefits can be realized by committing to running just 30 minutes a day a few days a week. Whatever your goals may be, a daily run can be enlightening, inspiring an epiphany even within a few miles. So intoxicating, in fact, are the effects that many people make running a habit and lifelong commitment even if the original goal for their running was short-term. So, what kind of runner are you? Well, you may be a different one tomorrow than you are today. Be open to that; whatever your goal, you might find yourself going from someone who just runs to someone who self-identifies as a Runner.

What Kind of Runner Are You?

For many, the lure of running at our best, discovering what lies inside us and what we are capable of, will always hold appeal. What kind of runners are these? The kind who are inspired and driven to train methodically for months for a single event and then run the very best that they are capable of from the starting line to the finish line. That's what "An Olympian's Approach" is all about.

Can recreational runners truly train with an Olympic approach if they're not world-class athletes with the talent and ability to run at an international level? Yes, they can. Believe it or not, essentially what goes into training as a committed enthusiast runner physically, mentally, and emotionally is the same as for elite runners. No matter your age, your experience, or your cumulative talent package, you can train like an Olympian if you fully commit to it.

The principles outlined in this book are universal, even if the end goals might be different. How you feel training by these principles—for example, the satisfaction of achieving goals; the ups and downs that come with training; the myriad feelings before, during, and after a race—is similar for all runners who follow this approach.

> *Running can't be simply something you do. It has to be part of who you are.*

You might once have had high aspirations as a runner but for one reason or another haven't put yourself in a position to fully commit to the sport or given yourself the opportunity or acquired the necessary tools to achieve excellence. As a coach, before I prescribe a training plan for age-group runners, I ask them to be honest with themselves and with me and to think hard about not only what kind of runner they have been but also what kind of runner they want to be. The two are sometimes the same but more often quite different.

I've found that, more often than not, most runners fall into one of four categories. While these categories are fairly well defined, any runner can aspire to move into a higher-level category if he or she is willing to commit to it.

The "I Want to Get Back into It" Runner

This runner is running little if at all but talks about it frequently with family, friends, and coworkers. He might catch the New York City Marathon on TV or get goose bumps watching inspirational Olympic highlights and then exclaim, "That's it! I need to get back in shape." This runner has a sincere interest in getting started but lacks a goal to keep motivated.

If this is you: Without a goal, it is all too easy to get derailed and slip back into complacency. Don't wait to get into shape or improve your fitness; register for a race as soon as possible, and you'll have all the motivation you need. Choose something that sounds fun or unique or features an attainable challenge, sign up, and start training according to the structure and insights provided in this book.

The Seasonal/Occasional Runner

This runner typically uses the annual 5K or 10K road race as the impetus to get out and start a standard 6- to 8-week training routine in order to avoid total agony and just complete the race. That's just enough time to see progress but not enough time and commitment to maximize race-ready fitness. After the race, this runner's training often becomes sporadic, and that new pair of running shoes ends up seeing more mileage going in and out of Starbucks.

If this is you: You'll benefit from picking more than one goal race. Pick three target races over a three- to six-month period, and hold yourself accountable for the consistent training and gradual improvement that this book can guide you through. You have proven that you can be consistent in spurts; just extend that over a longer period, and you'll be pleasantly surprised at your increased fitness.

The "Run Every Day at the Same Pace" Runner

This runner is committed and consistent, enjoys staying in shape, and recognizes the joy of running but struggles with implementing the necessary type of training to improve. The standard neighborhood loop at the standard pace becomes too easy and methodical and often lands this runner in a training rut or an extended plateau. Ongoing commitment and motivation to get out the door are not the issues here; the problem is lack of variety in training stimulus and perhaps lack of incentive to endure the discomfort necessary to improve.

If this is you: If you always run at the same pace, you can't expect to run any faster on race day. What you need is the new perspective on how to train that this book provides and a training plan, training group, or coach. That will help spice up your workouts with tempo, fartlek, and progression runs that use different paces with varying amounts of rest to stimulate higher levels of fitness. Assuming you already have a good aerobic base, you should see big gains within four to six weeks if you commit to the guidelines delineated in this book.

The Enthusiast/Lifelong Achieving Runner

This runner is committed and goal-oriented and enjoys the running lifestyle and camaraderie of training and racing. The aspects typically lacking are workout variety and individualization. Workouts are usually moderate tempo-paced efforts, just hard enough to feel challenging but without the true discomfort and suffering necessary to improve. This runner sometimes runs with a group but often runs too hard or too easy depending on the group dynamic and how she or he trains with others.

If this is you: You need to develop a specific training plan that complements a specific goal. Choose a race four to five months in the future. Before you start your training program, pick a reasonably aggressive time goal and then select a plan or coach that can help you achieve that goal. The more specific your goal, the more individualized your training needs to be. Write down your goals in a training log, and share them with your training group or coach as a means of holding yourself accountable.

———

You might waver between the lines of these types of runners, but the differences are tied largely to commitment, investment, and what you want to achieve. This book focuses on developing and maintaining runners of all kinds using an Olympic approach. While the committed runner will already have a comprehensive understanding of many of these principles, all levels of runners can benefit from the insights this book offers. No matter where you fall in that spectrum, there are ways to address your specific needs so that you can train better, get faster, and improve your running.

Committing to the Olympic Approach

A friend recently shared a story about two runner friends that really illustrated the difference between two types of runners and the differences in their levels of commitment and investment. One of the guys was a lifelong runner who ran consistently with no significant gaps in his routine and no lack of ongoing motivation. The second was an occasional runner who would run off and on depending on the season and what was going on in his life, but he lacked consistency. He would usually get pushed back into running following some kind of catalyst event, whether it was stepping on the bathroom scale and realizing he needed to lose a few pounds or signing up for the local Turkey Trot every Thanksgiving. He would also get bouts of personal inspiration from hearing his lifelong-runner friend relate stories about his recent marathons or from watching world-class runners competing in the Olympics or the Boston Marathon.

After a visit to his local running shop to get fitted with a new pair of shoes, he would once again be fired up and focused on getting fit. He would run several times a week for the first few weeks, but then the inevitable loss of momentum and dwindling excitement would set in because of soreness, fatigue, and a lack of motivation or a training plan. The seasonal runner asked the lifelong runner, "How do you do it? How do you keep motivated and stay with it?" The lifelong runner responded, "I don't know, really. If the weather isn't great, I take a day off and run the next day. If I feel like running a little longer, I do. If I feel like running a little quicker, I do. I honestly don't think about it much. I'm just a runner, I guess. That's just who I am."

To properly follow an Olympic approach, running can't be simply something you do. It has to be part of who you are—an important piece of your essence that is prudently and effectively woven into the fabric of your entire life—if you want to adopt a lasting and enduring ability to see goals through to fruition on a regular basis. Furthermore, running should not be a chore, not something you dread or do out of an obligation to health or weight. In becoming part of who you are, it should also become something you look forward to. It's not easy. It takes time and consistency, and it also takes developing a mind-set that eliminates some of the excuses that people make when it comes to exercise. You have to get over the all-or-nothing mentality that is a stumbling block for many people. That's a burden that afflicts many recreational runners, and even some elite athletes.

Different things hinder and motivate different individuals. The key to progressing from your current situation and improving as a runner is being honest with yourself, finding out what those barriers and catalysts are, and then stepping out of your routine to pursue becoming the runner you want to be. From there, you can experience the joy and energy that come from creating and preparing for a running goal. My goal is to help you progress down that path and take the necessary steps to get you on your way to becoming a fitter, faster, and better runner.

– 2 –

PSYCHOLOGY FOR SUCCESS

Running may be one of the most basic forms of human movement, but to do it well and run with performance-oriented results takes considerable commitment, training, and skill development, not just physically but also mentally.

Although running can lead to amazing breakthroughs and life-changing moments, it can also be a frustrating pursuit at times, no matter what your level or your goals. Fatigue, injuries, less-than-optimal results, the whirlwind of everyday life, and other challenges can limit your fitness, slow your development, and dampen your enthusiasm. No runner is immune to those types of trials and tribulations. Whether you're an Olympic hopeful, a dedicated enthusiast chasing a new half-marathon PR or trying to qualify for the Boston Marathon, or a new runner just getting started, things are bound to temporarily get in the way of your progress.

But runners can develop the mental skill set to help them get past obstacles, continue their pursuit of their ultimate running goals, and foster a competitive edge. That competitive drive, which varies in intensity among individuals, is a profound force that can elevate performance and allow you to go beyond your comfort zone, but it must be tempered with the right mental perspective in order to keep workout efforts in check and also maximize race performance. I was fortunate to reach the highest level of running in my career—including twice running in the Olympics—but I couldn't have done it without understanding and applying what I call a psychology of success. That ability did not happen overnight; it takes time to gain an Olympic mind-set. I learned, honed, and applied various mental tactics throughout my career. Indeed, my ability to be a good student of the psychological aspect of running probably salvaged my career many times.

Finding Motivation

My learning started early. I found myself at an all-time low point with my running early in my college career and was seriously contemplating quitting the sport, dropping out of the University of Colorado, and heading home to Texas to figure out what I was going to do with my life. It was about that time that I first started to learn about the psychology of running.

My challenges began just a few weeks into my freshman year in the fall of 1991. I had entered college as a high school All-American, but my development to that point had been based largely on my physical talent alone. The psychological side of my training was undeveloped. That fall I was injured with a bad case of iliotibial band syndrome, lateral knee pain caused by tightness in the thick band of fascia that extends from the pelvis to the lower part of the knee. It can lead to excruciating pain, so intense that it is impossible to run.

After hours of physical therapy in the training room, my left knee finally got better by December (after the cross country season had ended), but after six weeks of running, my right knee started hurting in the same spot. I wound up missing the entire track season of my freshman year. It was far from how I had expected things to go.

Although I was healthy and fit heading into my sophomore year, disappointment continued. I was running well, but then I was involved in a freak accident while moving a huge log during a volunteer project. It slipped and dropped directly on my right thigh, crushing one of the quad muscles in that leg. Why someone with my spindly physique was moving logs in the first place is a long story, but I wound up missing three weeks, and it cost me another cross country season. By early 1993, when track season was getting under way and many of my teammates had experienced two good years of racing, I was seriously questioning my desire to stay in Boulder and run at the college level. I had essentially missed a year and a half, and my confidence was completely shot. I had lost belief in my ability, and my resilience to push through to get back to a high level was buried.

Fortunately CU's head coach at the time, Jerry Quiller (or "Coach Q," as he was known), sensed that I needed a change and had the foresight and selflessness to assign me to work with the new volunteer assistant coach, Mark Wetmore. It takes a unique individual who has the athlete's best interest at heart to allow a new coach to take over a talented (if struggling) athlete. I'm grateful for Coach Q's generosity and wisdom to this day.

Mark was not new to coaching, but he was new to Boulder and ready and willing to do whatever it took to be a part of the program. He took a desk job answering phones because that position allowed him to get out by 2 p.m. to oversee our workouts. That first semester with our team, he was an unpaid volunteer, which meant he would have to drive himself to our track meets and pay for all of his expenses. He would load up his Subaru Brat and drive 10 hours for some rinky-dink indoor meet in Nebraska or Iowa or Kansas. His commitment to our small, tight-knit group of distance runners made a massive impression on me and fanned the flame of desire.

I was one of Coach Wetmore's first athletes at CU. At the time we began working together, I believed I had the talent necessary to compete at the NCAA Division I level but desperately needed to get back on track mentally and rekindle my drive. Under Wetmore's tutelage—which included both physical training and numerous mental coaching tactics—I started to develop a stronger mental skill set; concurrently (and not surprisingly), my belief in my ability and commitment to reaching my potential returned, stronger than ever. He worked hard to help me regain my confidence, refocus my goals, and reinstate my belief in my ability to accomplish those goals. A lot had to do with trusting in my preparation and understanding the training program he was administering for me. After four months of working with Coach Wetmore, I was healthy and fit and ran the equivalent of a 4-minute mile on the track.

It took time, however, for Mark to figure out the best ways to motivate me. I recall one afternoon after our daily practice, a few teammates and I were doing a post-run stretching routine in the field-house and talking about what I hoped to accomplish that season. After my teammates cleared out, Coach Wetmore said to me, "Your name used to be in ink around here, and now it's in pencil. Everyone doubts your ability, and you have to earn it back." It was a bold statement, meant to get me fired up. Wetmore had already established himself as a great storyteller, and, with a master's degree in sports psychology, he was skilled at reading his athletes. But we had only been working together for a few weeks, and he had not fully grasped the type of athlete I was. To his credit, that kind of tactic works well with many athletes, but proving naysayers wrong has never given me the motivation to run faster or better. I did not worry much over what other people felt about my running talent or my results. But at that moment, Wetmore was merely testing the waters to see how I would react and, in doing so, learning more about what made me tick.

Another common motivator for many athletes is trauma. A high number of elite runners have been through some kind of trauma, which serves as a catalyst for the motivation to compete and to win. The anger often associated with trauma can be a great psychological resource for many athletes and is often the added ingredient that spurs them to push to a higher level. This was not the case for me, however, as Coach Wetmore soon discovered.

To reach our potential, we must find our personal source of motivation, of desire, passion, and determination.

I remember I was training for the indoor track season when I realized that the NCAA indoor national championship meet was going to fall on the same weekend as my brother's wedding. I mentioned this to Coach Wetmore after I had qualified for nationals in the 3,000-meter run a few weeks earlier at a meet in Boston. He was floored when I told him with little emotion that I was going to have to miss the championships to be at the wedding. It was a nonissue in my mind. Family is important to me, and missing the NCAA indoor meet was not something I would lose any sleep over. There would be other races.

Understandably, Coach Wetmore didn't want me to miss an opportunity to compete at the national level and take what he viewed as a vital step in my progression. He came up with the idea to have me try to earn a qualifying time in the 5,000-meter run because the NCAA 5K race was scheduled for Friday evening. If I could qualify in the ensuing few weeks, I would be able to travel with the team to Indianapolis on Thursday, run my race on Friday, and then fly out on Saturday morning in time for the wedding festivities. It was a clever plan, one I had not considered, as I had trained for and raced the 1,500-meter almost exclusively during the previous outdoor season and had run only a few 3,000-meter races indoors.

The plan involved going to Iowa State by myself to run a "last-chance" meet to qualify for nationals in the 5,000, and it came with several logistical complications. Just before my trip, in the midst of discussing the details and my desire to go to my brother's wedding, Coach Wetmore said, "Alan, you need more trauma in your life." He knew I came from a stable home, that my folks were happily married, and that they were very supportive of my running.

Dig hard to find out where your desire really comes from.

He was right; I didn't have great trauma in my life. I did not have the kind of troubles that might have served as another level of motivation or incentive to become a great runner. Mark did not doubt that I had the talent to progress as a runner, but he was worried about my desire. Desire is something you can't teach; it comes from within—a willingness to fight for every second; to face your fears; to push beyond your limits; to never give up; and, figuratively speaking, to run your competitors into the ground. It is imperative to a professional running career. My nonchalant attitude toward missing a national meet for my brother's wedding suggested to him that I did not have what it took emotionally, that I lacked desire to be the best.

He may not have been correct about what motivated me, but what he knew then, and what I know now, is that it's crucial to understand what does motivate you as a runner and what kind of stimulus you react to best. We're all different, with different idiosyncrasies. Figuring out what drives you as a runner is key. Trauma didn't motivate me; showmanship didn't either. Pursuing excellence did.

To reach our potential, we must find our personal source of motivation, of desire, passion, and determination. I could not dig up any deep-rooted anger or life-altering trauma, like some athletes. I could not call on a deep pain, hurt from my childhood, abandonment, or other demons to fuel my running. Instead, I dug deep into my own psychological toolbox. I didn't find my motivation in anger or vengeance—but I found it, and that's what matters.

I ran a 13:53 at that last-chance meet in Iowa, set a school record, and qualified for nationals. At nationals, I finished as an All-American, and I had a wonderful time at my brother's wedding, too.

Six Steps to Developing a Psychology of Success

STEP 1: Recognize Your Incentive

If you're reading this book, there is a good chance that you are motivated to improve as a runner, want to learn how to train better, are open to making adjustments, and want to pursue your running goals to the fullest. Now you've got to come to grips with why you're doing it. What is your source of motivation? What does your desire to run the best you possibly can stem from? There are no right or wrong answers, but it takes honest introspection to determine why you want to run. You can't pretend to be someone you are not, physically, mentally, or emotionally. I could not pretend to run out of anger or fabricate a desire to beat my competition out of spite that they even thought they could beat me. Be real about who you are and what drives you.

Before you dive into training, recognize and embrace the incentive. After all, it is that singular motivating factor that you will fall back on when the training gets hard, when you start to lose some of that initial excitement and motivation, when you get into a training rut, or when the weather is bad and you don't feel like getting out there. Why do you want to go through all that is necessary to reach your goal? Is it out of joy? Anger? Disappointment? Loss? Faith? Need for freedom? Desire for attention? Without a true and clear understanding of your primary incentive, you may fall short of your ultimate potential. This is not meant to put you through a therapy session but rather just an exercise to gain a realistic understanding about why you're pursuing your running goals.

For some, the motivation is crystal clear. Some of the greatest athletes on the planet run to escape poverty, using the financial incentives of running fast to create life-altering changes in their future economic status. Most runners, however—whether at the high school, college, or recreational level—will never pursue running as a profession for monetary gain. To achieve your best as a runner, you have to dig hard to find out where your desire really comes from.

My own incentive was always centered on an unwavering pursuit of excellence. I knew I had a gift for running, and I wanted to get at every single ounce of my talent. I wanted the assurance that I had accomplished all that was physically and emotionally possible. In order to honor that gift, I had to see how good I could get, and after my first year and a half of college I never again doubted that I was going to see it all the way through.

I also liked that what I was doing was unconventional and that not many people could do it (or wanted to do it). And I liked the fact that running's noteworthy accomplishments were so quantifiable. I was competitive, and when I was side by side with other runners with a lap to go, I wanted to win. I wanted to win not out of distaste for my competitors but because I wanted to achieve excellence. Winning was proof that I was getting the most out of my talent.

To reach your full potential as a runner and achieve your short- and long-term goals, explore what motivates you. Being honest about your desire and true to your incentive will lead to your best performances.

STEP 2: Know What You Want to Accomplish

The next phase in ensuring that your psychology is aligned with success is having a clear understanding of what you want to accomplish as a runner—the end goal. For some runners, this is second nature—you

Think Radically

Sometimes you need to think outside the box to find what motivates you and to pursue your running goals to the fullest. As a senior in high school in El Paso, Texas, I made a very unconventional decision about my running future.

Until this point, I had run very well in high school and accomplished some major milestones. As a sophomore, I won the Texas 5A State Championships in the 1,600-meter and the 3,200-meter runs, winning each race with a final sprint down the homestretch. My junior year I won the state cross country meet in the fall and repeated as 1,600-meter champion on the track in the spring. By that point, although I had run a 4:12 PR in the mile, I still felt I had fallen short of my potential. The cross country season of my senior year included winning the state meet and culminated with a fourth-place finish in the national high school cross country championships in San Diego.

At the time, the championship event was called the Kinney Cross Country National Championships. The Kinney Shoe Corporation owned the Kinney Shoe brand as well as the Foot Locker chain of athletic shoe stores. It hosted national cross country championships each year in the United States, including qualifying meets in four regions around the country. I qualified by finishing fourth at the South Regional meet before placing fourth at the national meet. This was an important step for me. I established that I was one of the best high school runners not only in my state but in the country. I demonstrated that I could run well when it counted at the biggest meet of the year. I'll never forget the race director, Max Mayo, telling me, "You are going to surprise a lot of

continued >

people today," as he was about to introduce me at the starting line. I suppose he was right.

Running well there intensified my belief in what I could do and exposed for me even more fully my desire to get the most out of my talent. But I was in a tough situation, caught between my club coach, Sam Walker, who I believed was helping me progress as a runner, and my high school coaches, who felt I was not committed to the program, to the team, and to their coaching. They felt that if I fully committed, they could coach me to great things. Sam, on the other hand, felt that their record with previous athletes proved they did not have the coaching capabilities to maximize my performance. He pointedly asked me, "Why is the school record in the mile still at 4:20 from 15 years earlier?" This was tough to handle as a young adult. I wanted to run for the school with my friends and classmates and compete in big meets such as the Texas State Championships, but I also believed that Sam understood me and knew what I needed to do to continue to develop. I knew that both the school coaches and Sam had my best interests in mind, and I tried hard to determine what would most help me be true to my desire to honor the talent I knew I had. Trying to balance the school program with a club coach was not working. I was not running free; I was running with doubts in my preparation, doubts in my incentive because I felt I was being held back.

As a result, I made the unpopular decision to not run for my high school during my senior year. Quitting your high school team when you are the top runner in the state and one of the top runners in the nation doesn't go over very well. This was the year to set new records, to win more state championships, or even to go undefeated. But none of that was important to me. What was important was seeing how fast I could run without having to juggle both coaching scenarios, without the burden of having to do the workout with the team some days and other days to sneak off for a secret session with Sam. By not running for my high school program, I could race free from distraction and with a clear incentive.

That spring, under Sam's guidance, I raced in some open college meets as a raw and unrefined 18-year-old. I ran in a basic singlet with the club name "Independent Athletics" ironed on the front. It was a fitting name for my current situation. That spring helped propel my running in more ways than one. University of Texas–El Paso (UTEP) had been one of the first colleges to recruit foreign athletes from Africa, guys such as Suleiman Nyambui and Gidamis Shahanga from Tanzania, Michael Musyoki and Wilson Waigwa from Kenya, and others. Many of these athletes were still in El Paso when I was in middle school and high school, and by my senior year, they were in the twilight of their careers. I had heard stories of their training, had run on the same loops as they did, had done runs that were named after them. At the time, Sam was on a team with many of these great runners, and much of his training philosophy was honed by learning from the African runners.

I recall one memorable night in which Nyambui, a seven-time NCAA champion in college and 1980 Olympic silver medalist in the 5,000, organized a 3,000-meter race on the UTEP track. He invited some training mates and countrymen to compete, including the great Henry Rono, who was living in Albuquerque at the time. In 1978, Rono, then a student-athlete at Washington State University, had set world records in four different events in a span of just 81 days.

continued >

The Henry Rono I was racing against was certainly not that same athlete, but as an 18-year-old, to even be able to toe the line with a legend was something very special. Waigwa was making a comeback as a masters athlete, and Nyambui was just finishing his career around the age of 37 after having become a marathoner late in his career. I finished second in that race behind Nyambui, but much more important than the result was the profound experience of being exposed to such seasoned runners. This was the beginning of expanding my mind-set to include running at a much higher level.

On another occasion, I ran a 1,500-meter race against Nyambui and a few other runners in Las Cruces, New Mexico. In that race, I was tucked in behind Nyambui and fighting with everything I had to hold on from the starting gun. I knew we were on a solid pace, but all I was focused on was staying with Nyambui. With 500 meters to go, he started to pull away, but when he got about 10 meters up on me, he looked back and said, "Come! Come!" He slowed slightly to allow me to get back on his heels, and I immediately found a new level of motivation to accelerate and push harder to stay with him. I was able to hang right with him for another 200 meters, and with 100 meters to go, I ended up passing him and sprinting down the homestretch to win the small yet significant invitational. A few days later, Nyambui stopped by Sam's house, handed him a 20-ounce steak, and said, "Give it to the boy."

Later that spring, I drove with my parents, Sam, and a high school friend in a rented minivan to Tucson, Arizona, where I was entered in a 1,500-meter race in a twilight meet at the University of Arizona. We chose that larger college meet in the hope that I would get pulled to a fast time against a higher level of competition. Running with an unbridled joy that I had lacked for most of my high school years, I positioned myself right behind the leaders for the first lap and a half. When the pace started to lag, without hesitation I took the lead. Even as a teenager, I trusted how I felt while I was racing, and that night I had no fear of leading the race and knew I could maintain my effort. I held the lead all the way to the finish, bettering the field by some 60 meters. My time, 3:50.7, roughly the equivalent of a 4:05 mile, was the top high school time in the country for 1991. A University of Colorado assistant coach happened to be at the meet and watched my race unfold. He relayed my tactics and results back to Coach Q, and it helped solidify a full-scholarship offer to continue my running career in Boulder.

No longer was I having to disguise or compromise my incentive. I wanted to run fast times and pursue excellence to the fullest without being limited by coaching conflicts. I wasn't motivated by simply winning more high school races; I knew I was ready for the next level and finally felt free to run to my potential.

know exactly why you are putting yourself through the rigors of training and racing. Others find it harder to nail down clear goals or have never tried to do so. You have to eliminate confusion or vagueness before you get started so that your focus is clear.

Qualifying for the Boston Marathon is a focused, clear goal. Vague statements such as "I just want to finish well" or "I want to get fit" or "I want to run fast" are not. Those statements might be true, but they're not ultimate goals. Choose specific goals that are important to you. In this way, you will create a laser-sharp focus and achieve the best possible results.

Don't be swayed by peers or friends or training partners. Instead, think about what will give you the continual motivation to see your goals come to fruition. Focusing on a specific time for race distances is a good, clear goal, but it's important that your goals be both realistic and challenging—not too easy or too hard to attain. Narrow in on your race goal based on previous efforts, training, and running history. These are all good indicators of what is realistic.

For example, if you've only run one or two marathons, and your training has been spotty or unfocused up to now, chances are you can cut a lot of time in your next marathon if you're committing to better training and following an Olympic approach. If, say, you have a 3:48 marathon PR and you've never averaged more than 35 miles per week and rarely done advanced workouts, then there's a good chance you can make big gains in your next marathon training program. But aiming for a time that is considerably faster than your PR—say, 3:20 to 3:25—is a goal that must be tempered by many variables, including your current fitness level, the commitment you'll honestly make to your training, your past athletic history, and your age.

If you've run several marathons and trained well in the past but always seemed to run in the same range—say, 3:05 to 3:10—then you might consider shooting for a more moderate goal of breaking 3:00. The faster you get, the harder it is to make significant time reductions. Also, age can play a factor. Generally speaking, the older you get, the harder it is to reach times you might have run when you were 5 or 10 years younger.

The challenge in setting goals tied to race times is ensuring that they are realistic and properly gauged against these and other factors. Working with a coach who knows your running history, understands your athletic makeup, and has an idea about what kind of training you'll be doing can help refine goals related to race times.

You need to think through not only your long-term goals but also those in the immediate and near future as you build up to those larger goals. Your goals will help dictate how you train. For example, whether your ultimate goal is to run a 3:35 or a 2:40 marathon, you'll have to plan your weekly mileage volume during your base phase accordingly, and your goal will also dictate the length and pace of your tempo runs and long race-pace runs. Specific training goals are an integral part of a proper training program.

As I mentioned in the introduction to this book, as a young high school runner I wrote on a slip of paper that I wanted to make the U.S. Olympic Team. Writing specific goals down might seem inconsequential or unrealistic—perhaps even silly. But naming your goal and writing it down are very real steps toward psychologically committing to and investing in achieving that goal.

Today many runners are instructed to focus on more general achievements. But I believe that clearly defining what you want to accomplish is extremely important. The reality is that writing down your specific goals makes them more real, more important, more significant, more tangible—and thus more achievable.

Let's be honest, the essence of performance-oriented running—trying to get from one place to another as quickly as you can while suffering immensely in the process—is really kind of silly and somewhat insignificant. I mean, there's no real point to making yourself run fast over an otherwise arbitrary course from Point A to Point B unless it means something to you. (The same can be said about just about any sport if you look at it that way.) That's precisely why you have to create your own personal significance if you want to accomplish your specific goals.

Your goals and aspirations are really important only to you, so you need to own them and live by them. Write them down in a notebook, on a calendar, on your smartphone. Pick the top five things you want to accomplish for a given year or training period. These can be time goals, placing goals, qualifying marks, age-group accomplishments, records, or new personal bests. These goals should be something to reach for but not unattainable—lofty yet realistic. Writing them down gives you a reference point, a reminder that this is important to you, and will allow you to reflect back on and rekindle your baseline motivation. It's normal to lose enthusiasm during the course of your training, so having your goals written down can be a vital tool to refocus and constantly remind you of your ultimate purpose.

STEP 3: Commit to Achieving Your Goals

Now that you are clear on what it is you want to accomplish, you have to make the commitment, before you even get into the training, that you will do everything in your power to achieve these goals. This may sound extreme or even obsessive, but if you want to achieve something significant, something lofty, then you must have a clear and unwavering commitment from the onset. That includes developing or following a plan, making the time, and doing the work to make it all happen.

This book details an Olympian's approach to running, and one thing Olympic athletes of all disciplines share is this unwavering commitment to the pursuit of their goals. They're undeterred in their belief that they will accomplish what they set out to achieve. This does not mean that high-level athletes do not have moments of doubt or at times lack self-discipline or desire. They also have occasions when they fail and feel the unmistakable pain of disappointment. Everyone experiences those emotions from time to time. The difference is that high-level athletes do not let those situations and variables overpower their desire to succeed.

In the fall of 2007, I was assisting U.S. Olympic hopeful and former University of Colorado All-American runner Jorge Torres with a few workouts. He was working with Coach Steve Jones, a legendary runner who formerly held the world record in the marathon. Up to that point, Jorge had been an improving national-class runner who had won an NCAA cross country championship and qualified to represent the

United States in one world championship. He had posted some very good times in the 10,000 and was certainly a top contender to make the 2008 U.S. Olympic team, but he wasn't a shoo-in by any means.

One morning after a workout, Jorge and I were talking, and the topic of the following summer's U.S. Olympic Trials came up. I was surprised to hear in his tone a distinct hesitation and lack of certainty in his ability to make the team. Although he said he was confident he could make the team based on his 2007 performances, he did not come across as being fully committed emotionally to those words. Subtle clues in his word choices when talking about his goals revealed that he lacked conviction. He also admitted that he lacked focus, often allowing the chance to go golfing or work on projects around the house interrupt his training and, more importantly, distract from his commitment. To my mind, this was not a psychology for success. What he needed was an unwavering belief that he would make that team, a rock-solid belief in himself and his ability to qualify, and the commitment to do everything it would take to make it happen. I told him, "You have to decide today, right here, that you are going to make that team—that nothing is going to deter your commitment and focus on that goal. No injuries, illness, distractions, or anything else are going to keep you from making that team." I wasn't criticizing him but rather offering what I hoped was constructive motivation based on my experiences in training for the Olympic Trials as well as what I had seen among high-level international runners.

For American runners, the U.S. Olympic Trials are unlike any other race of their career. The pressure to perform is monumental because the trials are a one-shot deal every four years. Either you run well and make the team, or you miss out and wait four more years for another chance. Jorge was an excellent competitor and knew how to race tough and how to win. Mentally, he reasoned that he could certainly make the 2008 U.S. Olympic Team in the 10,000-meter run; however, he was not ready to make the emotional commitment to earning that spot on the team. He was flirting with the allure of letting himself slip into a vague commitment based on previous times and race results. No matter what level of runner you are, you cannot be less than 100 percent committed emotionally and expect to hold up when the pressure reaches a crescendo at an important target race. Instead of having a bold and confident determination, he was at risk of training for the Olympic Trials just to see where the chips would fall without the added expectation of accomplishing the larger goal.

Seven months later, Jorge ran a strong race in the Olympic Trials 10,000-meter final in Eugene, Oregon, and placed third with a 6-second cushion over the fourth-place runner. Despite a less-than-optimal buildup, his objective was unmistakable, and it was reflected in how he ran. There was no way he wasn't going to make the team that night. I am not suggesting that his success was based on our little talk, but he did tell me later that his mind-set changed that day and he spent the ensuing months adhering to an all-encompassing psychological commitment that complemented his physical abilities and preparation and allowed him to hone his objective with razor-sharp focus.

So how about you? Can you announce your specific goals right now—by writing them down—and are you willing to make both the mental and emotional commitment necessary to achieve those goals? You don't have to be an Olympic-caliber runner to make that commitment; without that kind of mental foundation and focus, you'll be hard-pressed to reach lofty goals, whatever they may be. In my experience, many runners can commit to the physical challenges—training, stretching, crosstraining, recovery, diet—but may fall short of making a full psychological commitment.

You must fine-tune your goals, state your intentions, and commit to them 100 percent. In doing so, you will create self-perpetuating momentum because once you commit, you are less likely to go back—only forward. You can't erase the fact that you've said you are going for it, nor will you be able to easily let yourself off the hook. Your goals become a powerful source of long-term motivation and allow you to use the passion connected to them to do the necessary work on a daily, weekly, and monthly basis.

That means there's no room for excuses, laziness, or self-doubt. Sure, you will have doubts, setbacks, and obstacles along the way. Every runner does. But continually invigorated by your goals and long-term progress and galvanized by your psychological commitment, you will be able to face those challenges head-on. Develop mantras to reinstate your commitment, and use verbal reinforcements to maintain your momentum. On a regular basis, remind yourself, "I am not going to let a fear of disappointment, a doubt in my ability, a fear of getting injured, or momentary lapses in focus stop me. I am ready to do what it takes to not get derailed and will maintain my consistent commitment to the goal." Or it can be something as simple as "I am physically strong, mentally powerful, and committed to my goals, and I can conquer minor setbacks along the way."

A continual reinstatement of a deep-rooted commitment will help you see goals through to fruition. This is not about being zealous and excitable—although enthusiasm is an important quality in a successful training period. Nor is a firm psychological commitment about being obsessive. Obsession is counterproductive because it can lead to getting distracted by things that are unimportant or out of your control, such as your competition, the weather, or the previous week's workout splits. Great athletes hone the skill of being 100 percent committed along with being flexible, being passionate in a way that is sustainable.

Committing is about keeping your eye on the prize while taking care of the business on a daily basis and doing all you can to make progress toward your stated goals.

STEP 4: Track Your Progress

The training diary is a psychological aspect of training that is often underestimated. Some runners brush off the idea of keeping a record of what they did in the buildup to a particular event. What's the point? they wonder. Meanwhile, other runners are in upload overload with GPS devices or other modern technological tools. Uploading data from your training has become a substitute for keeping a training diary. But, as in the case of writing down your goals, the practice of actually writing down your daily training activities can have a profound influence on your actually reaching them. Keeping a journal is another step in creating significance and psychological purpose for your running.

It is hard to remember the workouts you did last week, much less where you ran, what times you hit, or how you felt. By keeping a training log you not only create significance through an intentional act of recording your training but also have a record, an accurate account of what you are doing in preparation. You can refer back to any point in your training log to compare your workouts or simply to reflect on your training to build confidence.

Keeping a training log is something Sam taught me when I was a teenager. He required me to turn in my training log every few weeks. When I first started tracking my training, I would jot down short notes of where I ran and how far. I would add up my miles and cram a month onto one page. He quickly put a stop to that and laid out a template that I wound up using for 20 years. He had me put one week per page in a spiral notebook. Each week included the date, the workout or run for the day, total mileage, and specifics of the sessions. Information such as what intervals I did and where, how much rest I took, warm-up and cooldown, and how I felt was also included.

Being able to record a good hard training session in my log was very satisfying and created significance. Across my career, I accumulated years of data—information that I was able to refer back to for insight into what worked for me, what did not work, why I got injured, or when I was getting sick or anemic. This record ultimately provided me with a finishing touch of confidence leading into a race. I would reflect back on the training I had accomplished and quickly be reminded of how much solid work I had put in and how many good weeks of mileage, high-quality long runs, and tough sessions I had pushed through.

While keeping a log may not be something you've considered, I cannot stress enough how important it is. This is not a trivial act of just scribbling something down on paper right before your head hits the pillow. It is part of the process of building confidence and ascribing meaning to your daily efforts.

An online log is better than nothing, but I believe something important takes place in the physical act of handwriting information. It's similar to writing a letter versus typing an e-mail or text message. The old-fashioned writing process requires a higher level of engagement.

Habitually recording in a training log is much like keeping a diary or journal. People keep diaries and journals for reflection, and a training log is similar in many aspects. By reflecting on your training, you stay engaged and focused on not only the goal but also the process. If you have not kept one before, it may at first feel like homework or bad medicine. But once you get into the routine, I guarantee you will enjoy keeping track of your training and find satisfaction and reassurance in reviewing what you've written.

STEP 5: Keep It Fresh

Your incentive is clear, your goals are defined, you have made a conscious decision to meter your emotional intensity, and you have committed to keeping a training log. Now let's talk about how to get to the starting line feeling fresh, excited, and more confident than ever that you can accomplish your goals.

Even if you are a highly motivated and determined individual, there will be times during your training when you may find your enthusiasm waning and your mental strength getting flimsy. That's normal. All runners go through periods where they feel like they are physically or mentally flat and are merely slogging through workouts, going through the motions.

It is typical to have days or even weeks during which your drive to train is less than optimal and your ultimate goal is the furthest thing from your mind. In fact, if you don't have those periods during your training, you might not be working hard enough. Those flat periods come with hard training; cumulative fatigue; and variables such as weather, holidays, illness, and any number of other things that get in the way. But bouts of fatigue, lackluster motivation, or waning excitement, if allowed to fester, can start to chip away at your long-term mental outlook and compromise your psychological storehouse. I've witnessed—both as an athlete and as a coach—runners who start a training program with great intent and enthusiasm but little by little lose their desire. They lose connection with their motivation and stop caring about their ultimate goal or wind up operating with half the inspiration they had when they started. The fire goes out. And as you can expect, the end result is never what they had hoped for. We've all known runners like this; maybe you have been one yourself.

You need your fire to be burning hotter than ever as race day approaches so that when the time comes, you can push yourself beyond perceived physical and mental limits. Your mental approach to training should be modeled with that end goal in mind, which means implementing measures that allow you to stay mentally fresh and fired up throughout the training process. Strategies for staying mentally fresh include being clear about your priorities, maintaining a balanced (rather than obsessive) perspective, and doing your best to craft a lifestyle that fosters your training along with everything else.

A positive and focused mental approach will help you hurdle barriers that are bound to arise, such as dealing with the weather, combatting illness, training while traveling, and juggling family and work commitments. (I'll address these barriers in more detail in the next chapter, "Creating Balance.")

Rough patches happen. To prohibit them from becoming bigger problems, it is key to foster and maintain this strong and positive mental approach. Remember, training well takes not just physical exertion but mental exertion as well. And that's not altogether a bad thing; you need pressures and challenges to become mentally stronger, a tool in your toolbox that will serve you well on race day. However, your training should not leave you mentally flat come race time. Your objective is always to be ready when it counts, and being mentally fresh will help to make that possible.

STEP 6: Trust Your Instincts

Sometimes small decisions can affect the emotional toll of a given run or workout. Questions you ask yourself include: Where should I run a particular session? What loop should I choose on a given easy day? Should it be an out-and-back? Should I do the workout on the track, on the road, or on a trail? Should the run be hilly or flat? Should I run on a treadmill?

Choices you make depend on such variables as your schedule, the weather, or the requirements of the session. Trusting in your inclinations for a particular day (provided the decision does not jeopardize the productivity of the run or workout) will lift some of the mental burden associated with the actual training.

For example, I personally don't like out-and-back runs, especially for long runs. I would rather run four 5-mile loops than go out 10 miles, then turn around and come back. In college, we would run a horrific out-and-back on a canal path that Coach Wetmore named the "Certain Death" run. (There was a sign along the canal that boldly stated, "WARNING: Certain Death if Entered. Dangerous Current Present.")

We did some runs in college that were less than favorable, but this one in particular always left me mentally exhausted. Ten miles out, then turn around and head back to the car. No water, no Gatorade, alone after about 2 miles, and all at a 6-minute-mile pace. I felt like certain death every time we ran there, and I vowed to never run that path again after college. That run is a great example of how not every 20-mile run is created equal. For me, it added more mental load than necessary. Thus, when I was able to decide for myself, I tried to choose, whenever possible, what suited my mental disposition that day.

Once I left college and started training on my own, I would make the decision of where to run each day depending on how I felt emotionally. I would often leave my house not knowing what loop I wanted to run. I would get a few miles into the run and trust what felt right for that day: Go straight and do my loop called "Old Town," or turn left and head toward Coal Creek. Either run was fine for an easy day; it just came down to what I wanted to do that day. Whatever felt mentally easier is what I would choose. If it was windy, I knew which loop I could run where I wouldn't have to fight the wind. If it was snowy, I would choose the loop with the best footing.

One day, I had a track workout planned. It was in the middle of a particularly bad winter, and I had completed numerous sessions on the university indoor track. The indoor track was not ideal for multiple workouts in a given period. I decided to shovel the snow from lane one on the outdoor track and do my 200-meter repeats outside. Adding 45 minutes of shoveling was worth my time because it was so mentally refreshing to be on the outdoor track.

This is not an excuse to let yourself off the hook and avoid the hard efforts required in training. Much the opposite, actually. Taking the edge off psychologically whenever possible by making choices that reflect how you feel on a particular day will allow you to run with focus and intention during those hard workouts and will give you the mental bandwidth to dig deep without repercussions. There are certainly times when you have to just get the workout done because it is the type of session that requires a measured course, calls for being on the track, or has other constraints. But training is hard enough without making it harder by adding emotional stress. When you have a workout that can be accomplished in a variety of settings, choose with your mental disposition in mind.

The other time to trust your instincts is related to injury and illness, something I will discuss in more detail in Chapter 3. Too often athletes ignore clear cues. You wake up with an elevated heart rate or your throat is sore, and you know you are not feeling 100 percent. It is common to not want to deviate from the training program, and all too often athletes ignore those cues. It is an art form to recognize the difference between feeling a touch run-down or the normal aches and pains that accompany training hard and an illness that could become detrimental or a discomfort that could be an injury. These signals get easier to read over time, but some folks still choose to ignore them. In contrast, I have known athletes who take a few days off at any sign of discomfort, fatigue, or running nose. Be realistic and honest; your instincts about your own body and system are the best counsel.

− 3 −

CREATING
BALANCE

A few years ago, a friend of mine decided she wanted to run her first marathon. Her goal was to finish the marathon and enjoy the experience. Being a New Jersey native, she was drawn to the New York City Marathon. And understandably so—it's one of the world's most prestigious races, with an amazing course that winds through five boroughs of the city to a grand finish in Central Park. She was fortunate to get in via the lottery and started planning her preparation.

Being a somewhat new runner and having never trained for a marathon before, she sought the help of a local coach and training group. After building a nice base of fitness in the spring, she settled into a 16-week training program by the first week of July. She committed to the training with the end goal of her 26.2-mile marathon the first weekend in November. She had in place many of the right elements to assure her success: desire, perseverance, dedication, and a training program. What she was lacking, however, was balance, a not-uncommon situation among runners, and unfortunately, it ended up vastly diminishing her experience.

Training for an endurance event is not just about accomplishing a goal; it is also about the journey.

The main problem was that her training was forced upon her current lifestyle, obligations, and scheduling requirements. She allowed the training group's coach to dictate too many of the variables, which undermined her own dedication to the goal. Unfortunately, she did not choose a coach or group that were a good fit for her goals, and with this came continual and difficult compromises with her schedule as well as energy-sucking ongoing juggling to fit in the training.

Based on her goals, the training level was too aggressive, well above what she needed to complete a marathon and actually enjoy the process. Some of the many examples that wore her down and made for a less-than-ideal approach included long runs very early on the weekends for the sake of the group, hard sessions in inclement weather without concession, pushing through training during vacation, and a lack of compromise around her work obligations.

Despite all that, she did reach one goal and finished the New York City Marathon—but her experience was not a pleasant one. "I did not enjoy the race," she told me afterward. "All I did was put my head down, did not look to either side, heard nothing, felt nothing, and my entire focus was simply about finishing." Not surprisingly, although she has remained fit and active, she has not run since that marathon. It was all too much, and her training sucked the life out of what should have been an amazing, even a life-changing experience. Not only was her chance to enjoy a world-class event squandered, but the lasting satisfaction that comes with the process of preparation was compromised as well.

One of the best things about training for an endurance event such as a marathon is that it is not just about accomplishing a goal; it is also about the journey. Immense personal satisfaction can come from executing a great workout, taking a run on a beautiful day, breaking ground on snow-covered streets when no one else is out, exploring a new trail, running faster for a workout that you did weeks earlier at the same effort, or finishing a long run strong, knowing you could continue for 2 more miles if you wanted to. Equally meaningful satisfaction comes from a new level of fitness or the increased self-confidence derived from running. But those joys and gratifications can go unrecognized without balance, robbing you of a key part of the running experience.

I credit the consistency that I enjoyed throughout my career, performing at a high level year after year and continuing to improve, in large part to my ability to create an environment for success. I became very good at developing balance in my approach, and that allowed for sustainability. The Olympic approach is all about finding that correct balance so you can focus on completing the necessary training with the proper amount of mental output. If the training is forced into your schedule, as was the case with my friend, then it either won't be as productive as it could be, will drain the joy from it (thus zapping your desire to continue), or will require an unnecessary amount of mental energy.

There is a common misconception that training should be tough not only physically but also psychologically. Some runners feel it necessary to make the training harder mentally than it should be. I recall a friend telling me he got up very early every day, did 150 push-ups and other core strength exercises, and got out the door at dawn for his run. Though some runners may need to work out very early for scheduling reasons, he forced himself to do it merely because he thought it would make him tougher. In the end, all it really did was make him tired and cranky because he was continually sacrificing sleep. Don't make the training harder than it needs to be. Find your balance.

Developing an Environment for Success

During runs and workouts, you want your focus on the task at hand, not on what it took just to get out the door. If the setting is right, it is easy to focus on training. Getting the setting right is of course easier said than done. Many runners are so spent emotionally by the sacrifices made and juggling done just to get to the starting line that they cannot perform as well as possible. Having a clearly defined goal and a training plan in place to support that goal are imperative, but these are not all that is required. Endeavor to create an atmosphere that is free of unnecessary distraction and mental drainage.

The more significant the goal, the more careful you have to be in terms of psychological strain. Construct an atmosphere that makes training as easy as possible emotionally. You should enjoy training and allow it to exist only as a positive part of your life. By constructing an atmosphere that allows for the least amount of psychological strain, you free yourself to be mentally focused and physically as effective as possible.

Whatever your level of engagement in running, adhering to the principle of proper balance is critical. But how do you go about creating it? It begins with an understanding of the importance of what I call "training flow."

The Importance of Flow

The Russian psychologist Mihály Csíkszentmihályi famously defined "flow" as being "fully immersed in a feeling of energized focus, with full involvement and enjoyment in the process of the activity." Immersion, focus, involvement, and enjoyment are key components of having flow in your running. In sport, we often hear it called "being in the zone." But as it relates specifically to training, flow includes yet another crucial element: developing a systematic rhythm to your monthly, weekly, and daily routines.

It's critical that your training have this rhythm in order to be sustainable and ultimately successful. Anyone can train hard and adopt a mind-set that spurs on temporary motivation and a willingness to push hard through a particular workout for a few weeks or months. I am talking about more than being ready to train hard. Flow is a holistic concept that recognizes that every day has a purpose and a rhythm, and it incorporates large and small elements inclusive of both your training and your daily life. It's about having a sense of mindful presence when you look not only at how running fits into your life but also how each day's run or workout fits into your overall training plan. Each session needs to fit into the grand scheme, and no one part should be overemphasized. It's important to have a sense of presence every day and know what you're doing and why you're doing it as it relates to a bigger picture. You need to realize that a single day's activity—whether it is a long run, an easy recovery run, a grueling speed session, or a day of crosstraining or rest—is as important as that of every other day. Each activity plays a near-equal role in training, from hard work days to easy rest days. Understanding this rhythm helps you to focus on your tasks each day and also helps create and maintain a healthy, sustainable perspective.

Here are common scenarios that work against a sense of flow and rhythm. Do you recognize yourself in any of them?

Some runners turn workouts into a competition with others in their training group, basing their measurement of success on who finished ahead of whom in a workout or long run instead of how well they met that workout's prescribed goals.

Others focus too much on one or two days of the week—getting in a well-executed long progression run and pushing hard during a speed session—only to neglect recovery runs, active rest, or good sleep habits. They are in the bad habit of making the long run or weekly tempo run the main focus for their week and in doing so allowing the other five days of the week to become an afterthought.

Still others feel tired or experience a rough work day and either allow themselves to dog it during a tempo run or take several days off until work stress and sleep habits become normalized.

To reach your ultimate race goals, every aspect of your training must work in harmony. Temporary satisfaction or misguided competitive drive throws you out of balance and should be tempered if you hope to achieve your true potential. Pushing hard in a workout is great, but if you neglect post-run strides, cut the next day's workout short, or run too hard too often, you will not be able to achieve flow, that rhythmic accord that helps create balance and provides purpose and order to your training.

If you simply want to get back into shape or enjoy the simplicity of competition or an endorphin release, then pushing hard in workouts here and there or on the weekly long run is a great way to do so. If you have a specific goal, however, then your training must be intentional with a specific purpose for each day. In the chapter on training, we will explore how the various physiological elements work together on a weekly, monthly, and long-term basis to allow the body to be fully developed.

Finding flow from the beginning is critical. For one thing, establishing a rhythm allows you to better determine how you are going to feel each day. You may not always feel good, but you can at least be prepared for those days in the week where you don't feel as spry. Too, flow enables you to better wrap your head around the training. It is easy to feel overwhelmed when you start a training cycle, especially given all the other influences and variables in your life, such as work, family, and travel. When you go out and hit every workout hard or find yourself competing against training partners or obsessing over the number of miles in a long run or the pace you have to hit in your tempo, you can start to feel overwhelmed. You wonder, "How am I possibly going to keep this up week after week?" Flow helps you plan not just for a day but for the entire week and beyond, breaking your training down mentally into more manageable pieces.

It is a beautiful thing when a moderate 10-mile run physically, mentally, and emotionally feels like an easy 3-mile effort. Part of that has to do with advancing your training, but it also has to do with finding flow.

Once you develop flow, it can stay with you for the long term. For example, whenever I came off an extended break following a training period that led up to a big race, I was amazed at how uncomfortable I felt during a short, easy run. You know the feeling, right? A few weeks of less activity, and your aerobic base can start to dwindle. Truth be told, that easy 30-minute run would soon be shorter than my second run on any particular day. I rarely ran less than 5 miles at a time on a double-run day, and yet starting out with an easy 5 miles a few weeks after a big goal race always felt mentally like an uphill 15-miler on a windy day.

But that will not feel like a discouraging setback if you understand the rhythm of your training in the big picture and how your body adjusts following a rest period. As your body adapts, so too does your mind. Maintaining the mindful presence from your previous training period and carrying it over to your next one—even after you've lost some fitness and conditioning—will help get you through the rough periods of your new training program and keep your psychological and physiological systems in sync.

Finding Flow

So how do you develop flow in your training routine? You must establish a mind-set based on the rhythm of a training program in which every day has a specific purpose. Easy days, tempo runs, longer intervals, speed, the long run, mileage, tapering, rest—everything plays a role and is harmoniously interwoven into your weekly and monthly regimen. Allowing for a proper amount of time to build up also aids in this process and not only prevents many injuries but also lets you slowly work into the flow of training. How you sleep, how you maintain your diet, how you execute your fueling strategy, and how you implement your stretching routine all play into the development of flow. The process also involves prioritizing your time and making sacrifices when you must.

What gets in the way of flow are things like jumping into training without a plan, overemphasizing one element, pushing too hard in workout sessions, racing in practice, dogging your easy days, and a lack of mental acuity. You can't do everything and expect to do everything well. You can't limit your sleep, spend too many nights out with friends, or be a workaholic and expect to run with the proper level of intensity, focus, and effort.

Flow is about more than just training; it has to do with the overall balance in your life. It all starts with timing.

Timing Is Everything

A predictable schedule and training routine are the first steps in creating an environment for success and a platform that encourages flow. Lack of consistency makes it easy to get snarled up in all your other commitments or allows your daily run to become a cumbersome mental weight. There is nothing worse than having to put off your run and then having it hang over you in a negative way. Running should be our release, not a chore. Having a planned time each day for training helps eliminate lapses in self-discipline and keeps your training from becoming burdensome. The first step in creating the balance that leads to flow is choosing a time that fits your schedule and your temperament.

The training must suit your lifestyle and not be forced in where others think it should go. For many people, running must be done in the morning before the workday begins; some must get up as early as 4 a.m. to get a run in before morning obligations with the family, work, or commuting begins. For them, running at lunchtime might be a better option. Still others know they have time in the early evening, and for them this is the best option. The key is to be realistic.

As someone who transitioned from a full-time professional athlete to a full-time businessman with a young family, I have found that running in the morning is not feasible for me at this point in my life.

No One Gets By on Talent Alone

Having a systematic rhythm to training doesn't apply just to runners who train to run long distances. It applies to every athlete training his or her body for any sport. The world's most successful athletes in baseball, tennis, soccer, football, boxing, team handball, table tennis—whatever sport you can think of—have a sense of flow. There are always a few outliers, but they are the exceptions and not the rule.

I few years ago, I was in Fort Worth, Texas, visiting family during a holiday break, away from the harsh conditions of the Colorado winter. One morning, my wife and I went to a local college track to do a workout, and when we got there, we saw a big, fit, muscular guy doing what appeared to be old-school tire-dragging drills and plyometrics with a coach at his side. He was on the track before we got there and was still there two hours later as we were about to leave. We did our workouts, and after our cooldown we struck up a conversation with him during a break in his routine. Turned out it was Brad Hawpe, who was at the time the starting right fielder for the Colorado Rockies. He and his wife were from Fort Worth, and they spent their winters in Texas. He did some of his off-season training at Texas Christian University, including the workout we watched him do on the track that day.

Brad was interested to hear about our background as Olympic athletes, what we were training for, our college experiences, and what had led to our becoming full-time professional runners. I was interested in his training. Until that point I had never considered what sort of training a Major League Baseball player might do in the off-season. All I knew was what I read in the sports pages or saw on ESPN about how many players

continued >

would head to spring training dreadfully out of shape and over-weight. It turned out that Brad had a strict training plan laid out with a weekly plan and specific routine that incorporated strength, speed, agility, and endurance. He might have been 6 foot 2 and 200 pounds, but he looked lean, nimble, and fit when we saw him that December day.

After watching Brad work out and talking to him about his training and that of other players, I was extremely impressed. Not only was he athletically gifted, but his mentality and approach to his training matched his natural gifts. He defi-nitely had a sense of flow to his training, and each day clearly had a purpose. His training was not haphazard or overly focused on one area but had a holistic approach that included the entire off-season, with the goal of getting to spring ball in great overall condition and at a level of physical and mental fitness that he could maintain throughout the long season.

The 2007 season that had just ended had been stellar for him. He'd hit a career-high 29 home runs, helping the Rock-ies go on an amazing surge at the end of the regular season and play-offs to win the National League pennant and reach the World Series. In all, he played nine years in the majors—almost double the career length of the average player—and for a four-year stretch, 2006 through 2009, was one of the most productive right fielders in baseball. I am certain that his commitment to training, mental focus, and systematic flow and rhythm played a big role in that.

The overlap and similarities between his philosophy and mine were surprising to me at the time, and my respect for seasoned athletes in other sports was elevated by that interaction. It became clear to me that anyone who could remain at the highest level of any sport for a long period must understand this process and how to get into the rhythm of training both physically and mentally. Otherwise they would not make it that far and last so long. The bottom line is that no one can get by on natural talent alone.

Running during my lunch hour is my best option and one that I have grown accustomed to. I enjoy the break in the middle of the day to get out and exercise and don't feel the strain of getting up at the crack of dawn to go out the door. I know I wouldn't last more than a week if I had to wake up at 5 a.m. to get my run in. Couple that with the darkness of cold winter mornings, and I cringe just thinking about it. It all comes down to your personal preference and what is practical for you.

Running at a time that suits your temperament and schedule not only lessens the mental burden and gives you a greater chance to achieve flow, but it also helps to ensure predictability in how you feel. Running at approximately the same time each day allows your mind and body to get into a rhythm. Our bodies love routine. Taking a we'll-see, day-by-day approach makes it tough to predict how you are going to feel. Having some control over your timing helps you keep your focus on the workout at hand rather than on, say, the heat you didn't expect in the middle of the day because you never run at noon or the fact that you are uncomfortably full from dinner as you head out on the odd night run.

In addition, deciding on a time and embracing that it is your time to train lessens the chance of infringement by outside distractions or commitments. Plan parent-teacher conferences, business meetings, or other work and family obligations around your training time as much as is possible. In other words, treat your training time as one of your planned commitments, and don't compromise except when absolutely necessary. Holding fast to planned workout times reinforces your commitment and intention. Allowing your training time to be overrun by work or family obligations leads to inconsistency and disrupts balance. Does that mean you have to be a bit selfish about your time? Probably. But remind yourself that it is typically only an hour a day (perhaps longer on weekends), and the benefits are immense relative to the sacrifices you are making. Remember, even during extremely busy periods of your life, it is unlikely that you'll ever feel more stressed after you return from a run. Rather, your daily run often gives you time to clear your head, think rationally, and come to a greater understanding of stressors in your life. In contrast, missing your planned running time because of a work, family, or personal commitment can cause anxiety and break down and erode your dedication to running.

When I was training as a full-time athlete, my entire day was planned around my workouts—running two times a day, doing strength and core sessions, getting massage or physical therapy treatments, and occasionally doing crosstraining exercises—and although finding the time was less of an issue, I still approached each day very seriously. Elite runners who are training full time have different obligations, but the champion principles of commitment, dedication, and time management apply just as much to a recreational runner who works a full-time job. Elite runners typically run twice a day, four to six days a week in order to achieve the necessary mileage for racing longer distances. I always ran my primary sessions in the morning, after my standard morning rituals and proper hydrating, and did not let other things get in the way. Delaying that first run session by even one hour—by doing tempting things such as reading the newspaper, answering e-mails, running errands, or relaxing at home—adds an element of burden to getting out the door. The point is that no matter whether you're a recreational runner with a full-time job or an aspiring elite runner or somewhere in between, you must take advantage of the window of time allotted to you. Delaying by 20 minutes or 3 hours for any reason chips away at your intent and shifts the focus of your run from something you were planning to do with gusto to something you do with less meaning or even dread.

How can you build that window of opportunity for yourself? Decide what time of day you can commit to with the least amount of compromise to your existing schedule, and don't allow that time to be disrespected by yourself or by others. This reinforces your intention to the training process and helps build consistency. Your training should not be a burden but should rather complement your existing schedule. Sacrifices are certainly required, but not so much that you are continually making changes in your life or forcing the training where it just does not fit. The less-than-stellar results that my friend experienced in her buildup to the New York marathon showcases how this approach can undermine your goal.

Training Alone Versus Group Training

For many runners, training with a group is an essential component of successful training. Indeed, many of the world's best distance runners train with other runners. Elite runners from Japan, Kenya, and Ethiopia have consistently achieved success with group training, and in recent years many top U.S. runners have returned to the group training model that flourished in the United States in the 1970s and early 1980s, when American runners achieved a high level of success in international competition.

For recreational runners, running clubs or specialty stores often have training groups that meet a few times a week for harder sessions and the weekly long run. Many runners benefit from a group dynamic because it makes the mental aspect easier; getting out the door to go push a hard workout is easier when you have a group to meet and also provides accountability, not to mention the added benefits of being around like-minded individuals and enjoying the camaraderie of others who share your passion.

For some runners, however, there is nothing quite as wonderful as running alone. Whether during long runs, easy runs, or even hard workouts, some people love and respect solitude.

I did both, always with an eye toward individualizing my approach to training. Once out of college, I did not train with one particular group regularly but rather used different groups or individuals to the benefit of my training and my psychological stimulus. I did not find it useful to take a generic approach in which an entire group performed the same workouts week in, week out. Nor did I wish my workouts to be adversely affected by other athletes and their training schedules.

For me, there was nothing worse than having someone racing me in practice who did 25 percent less mileage a week, took days off consistently, ran a significantly shorter long run, and was in essence fresh for workouts—and then felt the need to be up front pushing the pace. As soon as I graduated from college, I began to dictate my own schedule and align myself with others who I knew would complement my training.

Although I was self-coached and did a lot of my running alone, I also trained with Adam Goucher, Scott Larson, Pete Julian, Marc Davis, Mark Plaatjes, Mark Coogan, Keith Dowling, Shawn Found, Andrew Letherby, and many others along the way. There will always be some athletes who complement your style and approach better than others and some you simply enjoy running with. (In the next chapter, I'll highlight some of the cautions of training with others as it relates to intensity, and specifically some of my experiences doing hard workouts.) The model I adopted was based on the premise of using other athletes to elevate my productivity during workouts while at the same time eliminating some of the unnecessary anxiety and mental burden that can accompany training alone. My goal was always to make the training as mentally easy as possible while still getting the necessary physical work done.

The biggest benefit of group training comes during the hard sessions. Without question, running a hard session with a group allows for the opportunity to push just a little harder than you might alone. A group session can create a setting in which it is easier to achieve high-quality efforts, removing a large amount of the anxiety, dread, stress, or physical complacency of not running hard enough.

I've done many hard workouts in which I've thought, "I can't wait for this to be over." Doing some of my workouts in a group setting helped alleviate that stress before it elevated. That didn't always mean I would do the whole workout with the other athletes; sometimes I would simply warm up with the group or perform my own workout at the same time and place alongside the others. Just having a group at the track at the same time can take the edge off the workout mentally and provide enough distraction to not feel like a crazy person enduring this pursuit alone.

Another option I would often exercise was to integrate just a portion of a group's workout into my own session. For instance, if the others were doing 400-meter repeats at a similar pace to my 800-meter or 1,000-meter efforts, I would do the first lap with the group and keep going to finish the entire distance of my reps. At times that meant I would have to adjust the amount of rest between reps in order to be in line with the group's routine. But having the built-in support for some of my reps allowed me to have some great sessions doing workouts in this fashion.

Despite the many benefits of group training, I probably most enjoyed and appreciated running alone. Running solo on my easy days allowed me to pay closer attention to how I was feeling and ensure that I was recovering properly for the next sessions while at the same time not running too easy and missing the opportunity to gain a small aerobic benefit from the effort. Running with others on my easy days almost always included some kind of compromise of when and where the run would take place. In addition, it inevitably led to conversation for the duration of the run, which led to my heart rate being elevated and my pace slower. Sometimes a group even becomes a crutch, and you wind up taking on the habits of the group, some good but some bad. While having the accountability is great, you must take care to maintain your individual incentive and not lose your personal motivation or running identity.

In the end, there are benefits to running with a group as well as to running alone if both are done strategically. If you have only run alone to date, consider finding a group to share your passion and the ups and downs of training. If you tend to run with other athletes for every run, consider taking a step back from that. Running alone has its charms and benefits. It's a time when you can keep tabs on your physical self, but it's also a chance to reconnect to your psychological self. One of running's greatest benefits is the primal act of getting lost in thought, and that's nearly impossible in a group scenario.

Maintaining Balance When Life Gets in the Way

The first few years after graduating from college, I would often include one of Coach Wetmore's unique workouts that called for a 5-mile tempo run in the morning and then 16 × 300-meter repeats in the afternoon. The logic behind two hard sessions in one day was to stress the system in two distinct ways. I always enjoyed these workouts and usually felt really good during the second effort of the day. Your nervous system gets activated in the morning, as does your cardiovascular system, which makes the second effort much easier than one would expect. Also, since we usually did a tempo effort in the morning, coming back to do short intervals with generous recovery in the afternoon would not leave me very fatigued. The quick 300-meter repeats actually felt good and were not too mentally strenuous due to the shortness of the intervals.

On one occasion, deep in the Colorado winter, I had the two-in-one-day special on the docket only to wake up to snowy winter conditions

Running with Music

Running with music can be a good distraction, but it can defeat one of the purposes of running solo because it doesn't allow you to be alone with your thoughts. Running with music actually mimics some of the aspects of running with a group, adding a layer of complication and distraction that takes the focus off your running, lessens your ability to pay attention to your body, and can alter your pacing. (Just the act of finding your music player and headphones before your run, having songs that match your running rhythm, and controlling the song selection and volume during a run can add a layer of complication.)

Some runners say they simply cannot run without music. My advice to them is to keep it as simple as possible, relegate music to long runs or easy runs, and be vigilant that it does not compromise the daily running goals. I would also suggest that those runners make an effort to run without music once in a while, both to listen to their bodies and to try to develop a harmonious interaction between their physical movements and their psychological state of being. It takes getting used to, but you will be amazed after some practice at how much more in tune you are with the effort. Running with music tends to compromise the ability to achieve the flow state created by an uninhibited interaction between your senses— not only your hearing but also your sense of sight and the proprioceptive feel for the surface under your feet—and the environmental influences around you.

that were unfavorable for running outdoors. I was training with Marc Davis (a 1996 Olympian and former American-record holder for 2 miles on the track) and former college teammate Shawn Found (a sub-29-minute 10K runner) at the time. Because of the weather, we decided to flip the two workouts and run the 300-meter repeats on the indoor track at the University of Colorado in hopes that the sun would melt the snow to the point where we could run the tempo run that afternoon with good footing. After completing the 300s, we spent the next five hours eating, rehydrating, and resting our legs.

Training effectively is a delicate process of pushing hard and taking risks while complementing that intensity with recovery.

We reconvened at 4 p.m. to run the tempo run on the dirt roads around the Boulder Reservoir. We started our warm-up, and within 2 minutes we realized the slippery, ice- and snow-packed surfaces were going to be a huge challenge. The top layer had melted during the warmest part of the day, but by late afternoon, temperatures had dropped to 15 degrees and made everything very slick.

We discussed whether we should bag the workout or make it work. Since we were already out there, we decided to give it a try. I remembered that I had my racing spikes in the car, and it suddenly came to me that we could wear those on the icy dirt road. Racing spikes are designed to be used on a track surface, and although we have all used them for various cross country workouts and races on grass at times, this was no track, nor were there any grass or soft surfaces to be found. But in my mind, the idea of wearing spikes to run on ice for a 5-mile tempo run in 15-degree weather made perfect sense.

I made it through the out-and-back tempo run unscathed—barely—but it was not a wise choice. I could easily have ended my entire cross country season with one bad step. There are times when taking a risk is necessary to improve, and there are times when a prudent choice is in order. At that particular point in the season, skipping the second of two workouts in the same day on an icy death trap would have made good sense. It would have been smarter to go to the gym and run the tempo on the treadmill or do an altered version of the workout. I didn't want to do that because I was mentally prepared to do the workout and didn't want to feel like I was skimping in my preparation. That kind of mind-set can be dangerous because it leads to poor decisions. Having an approach anchored in common sense is always best. Sometimes things out of your control—like dangerously slick roads—come up, and you need to alter your training without considering the change a mental or physical setback of your ultimate goals.

Training effectively is a delicate process of pushing hard—harder than your body and mind often want to go—and taking risks while complementing that intensity with recovery. It takes honesty and perception every day, and it involves using your head and not just relying on your emotions to make a decision. Sometimes compromise is in order. The key question you have to ask yourself is whether the workout or run will set you back more than it will be of benefit. The biggest variables for most runners, regardless of ability or experience level, are weather, illness, travel, and family or work commitments.

Weather

You may have heard that running in harsh weather conditions makes you tougher. But does it? While there are times when you can gain a psychological edge by proving to yourself that you are mentally strong enough to run on a windy day or that you're not going to curtail a workout because of drizzle, trying to combat the elements often just breaks you down mentally and can lead to lingering ailments or even injuries.

Your training, if prescribed correctly, should be challenging enough without having to fight the weather. That doesn't mean that you can't run if the weather isn't ideal. But you don't always need to go head-to-head with it either. Mother Nature is a powerful and often relentless force. Yes, there is satisfaction in running in cold weather, completing a good workout on a windy day, or refusing to back down when the weather changes unexpectedly. But there is a big difference between dealing with the weather and fighting it. Dealing with it is empowering; fighting with it is draining.

The following scenarios provide some examples of fighting the weather versus making adaptations to deal with it.

Fighting it: You have planned a long run with a training partner on a standard loop in which you know the mile markers. But when the time comes to do the run, you find that the wind is blowing at 25 mph and gusting even higher. Instead of changing your plans, you head out with your partners and hope it won't be as bad as it seems. You get battered by the wind for two hours, and worse, you don't feel as strong as your training partner, which undermines your confidence and leaves you emotionally down in the dumps.

Dealing with it: Instead of starting a long run in miserably windy conditions, you and your training partner opt to either take a new route that is sheltered from the wind or delay the run for a few hours to see if conditions improve. This doesn't mean you are weak or lack toughness; it means you're smart and want to get the benefits of the long run without the detrimental side effects.

Fighting it: You have a tempo run planned that you normally run at lunchtime, but the weather ends up much warmer than expected. Defiantly, you head out in the heat of the day and run the workout as intended. You wind up cooked from your efforts, and the ensuing dehydration and fatigue take their toll over the next several days.

Dealing with it: Instead of pushing on through the heat, you consider pushing your workout back a day or shifting the session until later that afternoon, when it is cooler. You get the benefits of running at a sustained tempo pace without the lingering negative effects brought on by the heat.

Fighting it: You wake up on a morning when you have a speed workout planned to find that a few inches of snow have fallen overnight. Trying to prove to yourself that you're tough enough to run in wintry weather, you forge ahead with the workout on your normal loop. You find yourself frustrated with the pacing of your intervals and irritated due to slipping around for an hour. You also put yourself at greater risk of injury from the unstable footing.

Dealing with it: You decide to either simulate the workout indoors on an indoor track or on a treadmill or bump the workout to the next day.

There are times to break from your routine and times to push onward. If unusual circumstances demand compromise, be creative with your training. Using a treadmill is a great alternative when dry ground and safe footing are not an option or when heavy winds make it impossible to run with a consistent gait. You will get a better workout on the treadmill than slipping around on snow-covered trails or being battered by the wind.

What's the bottom line? Don't consider the weather your enemy or an unnecessary stressor that is impeding all the progress you're making toward your ultimate goals. Yes, weather can be an obstacle and can change unexpectedly. Keep your perspective, and don't allow it to be more than a small variable, a temporary impediment to work around. By adapting your workouts with small adjustments or schedule changes, you can still maximize your training efforts, avoid injuries, and maintain your long-term psychological composure.

Illness

Running when you are sick isn't fun, nor does it allow for effective training. Your body is telling you it needs rest; you need to listen or suffer the consequences. When I pushed too hard in training, I would often become ill. Getting sick is sometimes an indication that you are training too hard, that you are pushing your body to the point of being more susceptible to illness. Or you might simply have picked up a bug. Either way, it's a good idea to rest and not push yourself too hard when you're not 100 percent.

When you feel awful, it is easy to take time off. The harder decision comes when you feel so-so—not great but not terrible. Training when you are ill often only extends your illness and in some cases can make it more severe. Too, jumping back into training too quickly following an illness, even if you might be at 80 or 90 percent of your normal health and energy levels, usually is not favorable to overall productivity in training. It is far better to rest for two or three more days, run easy or not at all, and skip the planned harder session before jumping back in.

If you don't follow a conservative approach and instead try to force yourself into action, you may find that your run is much more taxing than it should be. My own inclination was always to tough it out and just run even though I didn't feel great. I never wanted to lose physical momentum or feel like I was bowing out. But I strongly advise against that approach. Trust in your overall training, and know that your training plan is based on the entire plan, not just one week or a few days. Doing workouts when sick or when you are on the mend never leads to improved fitness. Nor will you lose fitness by missing a few days of training.

You've got to weigh the pros and cons and trust that you will bounce back if you take the extra day or days off. If missing one or two workouts during a week means you can come back healthy sooner, then this is the wisest course. If you simply must run to keep the psychological edge, then compromise by running very easy and shorter than planned. Or considering doing some gentle crosstraining that provides both physical and mental stimulus.

Travel

Travel is another area where you must be realistic about how your body reacts to going off its normal routine. With travel comes dehydration, fatigue, stiffness, and other less-than-ideal variables. The pressurized cabin of an airplane and lack of ability to stay properly hydrated do not lend to productive training at the end of a long day, nor does sitting for hours in a cramped airline seat, changing time zones, and altering your eating habits.

Traveling requires a lot of energy and focus even when a trip goes smoothly, let alone when it includes delays and other challenges. If you have a trip coming up and you know that running on your travel days will be touch and go, try to rearrange your training schedule several days out so you can accommodate a run before your flight and move your harder workouts to other days.

A bad combination is traveling and hard sessions. Getting in harder sessions on travel days is difficult to do effectively. You are better off getting up early the next day of your trip or cutting the workout altogether than running when your body is not ready. Even if you are psychologically ready, it usually does not make sense to push in this manner because of the emotional stress tied to both travel and harder workouts. Forcing the issue will likely only compromise future training sessions and possibly increase your fatigue and likelihood of getting sick.

A light shake-out run on a travel day is typically fine, but second sessions should be the exception. It is far better to take an extra half hour to get hydrated and do some light stretching than to run an easy half hour, then squeeze in a longer run or hard workout. The overall benefit does not outweigh the physical and mental burdens that accompany the trip.

Running while at your destination can also present challenges. You may be busy with work and other commitments that compromise your training plan. Or perhaps there is not an obvious place to run near your hotel. Think outside the box. Not every run when traveling will feel good or be perfect. Some may be on a treadmill, and some may be simply squeezed in when you get an opportunity.

If timing and routine are the most important aspects to consider when trying to create a high level of productivity, then traveling certainly hampers those things, forcing changes in sleep, hydration, diet, and training time and duration. The key is deciding whether a run or workout is critical to the overall plan or whether a small sacrifice is in order.

No one can make the decision of running while traveling better than you, which is why planning is critical. As you consider your trip, think through when you will best be able to run just as you would during a normal week. It may not come together perfectly, but it is much better to plan your schedule ahead of time and anticipate possible conflicts. A whimsical approach to training while traveling—or no approach at all—is no different than a lackluster approach at home.

Family/Work Commitments

As a husband, father of four young boys, and someone who works a full-time job along with coaching and writing on the side, I am very familiar with the delicate balance of life and how it affects training. This area is tough because it does not just affect you but has big implications for others as well. Illness, travel, or weather all have personal implications, but when it comes to family and work, other people with their own variables are typically involved. For that reason, this special consideration can be the most challenging of all.

Balancing work and family commitments with your running takes a high level of sensitivity, communication, and sometimes compromise. Work deadlines, meetings, conference calls, and management of other coworkers all play into the mix. Your children's school functions, parent-teacher meetings, concerts, recitals, sports, and homework likewise have implications for your schedule and training. Your particular set of circumstances is unique to you, and I would be out of place to suggest any specific solutions or ordering of priorities. What I will say is that you can probably do more than you think is possible, even amid what seems to be an impossibly complicated weekly schedule.

We all live busy lives, and certainly some people have less flexibility than others, but I believe there is always time to train. You can make time for things in life that are important to you. The secret lies in the scheduling, planning, and commitment. With proper scheduling, focused training amid even the most complicated schedules is very feasible.

When my wife, Shayne, and I were both training as full-time professional runners, we organized our days around our training. Naturally that became more challenging after we started a family. We still planned our days around training, but we also had to account for our children's needs and schedules. We talked about what worked best for each of us and came to the understanding that Shayne, who took on more child care responsibilities during the day, needed to run first because she could not delay her training even slightly without the burden of the running becoming very heavy. With that as our starting point, we planned our weekly schedule accordingly.

On our easy days, we would trade off, one of us taking care of our kiddos while the other ran. For harder running sessions, we arranged for the necessary child care so that Shayne and I could both train in the morning. I could not wait until 11 a.m. to get to the track to do a 6 × 1-mile workout or hard 1,000-meter repeats or a long tempo run. These sessions required increased focus and precision, and for me, postponing the effort until later into the morning would create an unnecessary burden and ultimately a long-term drain.

It took some time, effort, and sacrifices, but we were able to find a good balance that helped maintain optimal training opportunities but also benefited our family. In fact, Shayne and I each ran many of our personal best times and enjoyed some of our best races after starting our family. This was partly due to our overall happiness and enjoyment of having children, but it also had to do with setting a realistic and sustainable schedule that allowed each of us to continue to flourish. Knowing your limitations and being honest about what you are capable of maintaining is vital. While some sacrifice is necessary, you have to be reasonable about the demands you place on yourself so that you can fully commit to the routine you develop. The time of day you choose to train is a simple yet very important part of finding a balanced approach.

Several years ago I had a business meeting with the then mayor of Tempe, Arizona, Hugh Hallman. We were discussing the Rock 'n' Roll Arizona Marathon, which finishes in Tempe. He had been running for only five years but had come to fully embrace the essence of running and the freedom, clarity of thought, and daily satisfaction of accomplishment it brought to his life. At the time we met, he was training to run a marathon and was leading a charity organization that had raised more than $300,000 through the Rock 'n' Roll event platform.

He met with me at 6 p.m. at a pub in downtown Tempe after a busy schedule of meetings. He graciously kept our meeting time, and we discussed all the event details as well as his involvement in running. He shared how he had gotten started and what type of training he was doing in his lead-up to the marathon. As we concluded our meeting, he told me he was going to meet his wife to do their evening run together.

I was amazed that he still had plans to run after what had surely been an exhausting day, but it was a good example of how he found balance in his life. He shared that he absolutely had to run, not only for his sanity but also because it was his time to connect with his wife and talk about their days. After they ran, he would go home and eat, shower, and work a few more hours before going to bed. Now, we are not all mayors of cities, and this is an extreme case of a chaotic schedule, but it shows that there is always time for your running. As long as you schedule for it and make it a priority, it can fit into any schedule.

– 4 –

EFFORT &
INTENSITY

There may be a fine line between a hard effort and an intense effort, but they are distinctly different concepts in running. A hard effort typically describes the physical output of a workout or run, while an intense effort relates to the mental or psychological approach. It takes time to learn how to execute a run or workout with awareness of each of those variables. My final season of collegiate cross country proved to be a wonderful teaching experience in how hard is too hard.

During my senior year, I started experimenting with my daily effort to test my physical limits. Up to this point, I was improving and training hard but had yet to fully test my threshold for hard training. Unfortunately, I wound up running with too much intensity on too many occasions. One such run occurred just two weeks before our NCAA regional meet in late October, at a point when long runs started to become less of the central focus of the week. Coach Wetmore typically decreased our mileage slightly in mid-October as we geared up for the NCAA championships in late November.

> *The difference between hard and intense is the mental approach.*

One Sunday, we were scheduled to run 15 miles at "the Grange," a rural location north of Boulder that started at an old barn with the words "Altona Grange" displayed on a faded sign on the side of the building. The runs there were all on rolling dirt roads and were particularly challenging due to the start and finish being situated at the highest point on the route. The first 6 miles were all downhill, followed by 3 miles on flat terrain and then 6 miles making our way back to the finish.

At the time, Coach Wetmore coached a handful of postcollegiate runners, including Craig Dickson, who had graduated from Adams State College in Alamosa, Colorado, and moved to Boulder to train with other U.S. Olympic Trials Marathon qualifiers. On this particular occasion, Craig brought a friend of his, Pat Porter, whom he knew from his days in Alamosa.

Porter was one of the most accomplished American distance runners of all time, especially when it came to running cross country. He won the U.S. championships a record eight times and finished among the top 10 at the World Cross Country Championships four times. He also made the 1984 and 1988 U.S. Olympic teams in the 10,000-meter run on the track, set a 10K world record on the roads, and earned a silver medal in an IAAF World Cup 10,000-meter race in Australia.

In 1995, Porter was 36 and making one last push to make the U.S. team for the 1996 Olympics in Atlanta. Along with some of the great Kenyan runners, Pat was a guy whom I had grown up admiring. As a kid, I had thumbtacked running-magazine covers with his picture to my bedroom wall. I was thrilled to see him get out of Craig's car. As I walked over, I whispered, "Is that Pat Porter?"

Mark went through the usual routine of explaining who was doing which route for the day, how many miles and how fast, and provided a short disclaimer about the upcoming regional race, cautioning us to stay under control. In my standard fashion, I was at my car removing the final layers of clothing and taking a few last gulps of water. As I approached, I noticed Mark and Adam Goucher talking. Mark said to me, "Forget regionals; it's today." Although he made the comment jokingly, there was a hint of seriousness, and Adam and I took it to heart. This day was going to be not only a hard effort but also an intense effort. Mark appreciated that Adam and I were very fit, and I suspect that he wanted to make a statement to Pat, to show one of America's greatest runners that the University of Colorado was no joke. We trained hard in Boulder. Mark knew it, Adam and I knew it, and we wanted to be sure Pat knew it.

As I said, the difference between hard and intense is the mental approach. A lot of workouts and long runs can be hard efforts, but adding the mental intensity can make them truly painful. The caution for any runner doing a run or workout is not to add so much intensity that you wind up running harder than what is called for. Adding too much intensity to a hard effort creates a pseudorace scenario that can put you in a physically depleted situation that can be hard to recover from—something I learned the hard way that day.

We started the 6-mile downhill portion of the run at our usual under-6-minute mile pace, but where this run differed from other times was over the next 9 miles. Instead of settling in during the flat section and maintaining over the final 6 miles back uphill, we pushed the pace. Adam and I were at the front, setting the tone and keeping the pressure on. We increased the pace to the 5:40-mile range and did not falter. There is a long climb from miles 10 to 11, and Pat, never having run the course before, asked, "How much farther?" He told us he didn't feel great and mentioned the fast pace. He started asking for mile splits to help quantify how fast we were running. Not knowing a course that you are running is difficult on several levels. He had no idea how much farther we had to go, something Adam and I used to our advantage.

Although we all rolled up the final hill together, Adam and I were in control of the pace and dynamics of the run and, to Mark's delight, looked strong as we finished, while Pat and Craig were noticeably spent. Pat was wiped out and talked for 15 minutes about how hard the run had been and how he had never done a long run like it before. He was interested to hear about Mark's training, and, as always, Mark was reserved in his divulgence. Craig later shared that Pat slept in the car on the way to the airport.

But there is more to the story, and therein lies the lesson. Without question, I ran that long run way too hard and felt the effects for weeks to come. It was clearly a case of competitive immaturity—not knowing enough to back off and run smart when it is warranted. Although I ran a good race at the regional meet two weeks later, finishing second behind Adam, I didn't feel great. Ten days after that, at the NCAA Championships on a chilly day in Ames, Iowa, I struggled. Although I still earned All-American status, I was far from my goal. I believed I was capable of finishing among the top-10 runners in the race, but I wound up placing 24th that day. (Adam placed sixth.) I won't say that one long run was the only cause, but, combined with other similar instances throughout the season, it caused me to run below my potential when it mattered most. It was one of many lessons I learned that season about how my body reacts to effort and intensity, and it certainly helped me down the road as a professional runner. I ultimately found a nice balance between hard and not too hard once I graduated from college and understood when each was appropriate in a given context. This was largely due to my honing the skill of perceived effort and, now out of college, having the freedom to remove myself from a group training environment as needed.

Some athletes never make those adjustments and wind up training too hard too often. Many runners—from the recreational level all the way up to world-class elites—push too hard when they should not

Competitive Training Partners

The dynamics of a training group or partnership are often quite varied because each runner brings a different set of skills and tendencies to long runs and workouts. Adam Goucher is one of the toughest runners I have ever met, trained with, or raced against. As teammates at the University of Colorado and regular training partners afterward, Adam and I logged many miles and hard workouts together.

Goucher was a three-time NCAA champion at the University of Colorado and a multiple-times U.S. champion and 2000 Olympian in the 5,000. He was also a training partner who had a propensity toward racing intensity during practice. He was self-admittedly an ultracompetitive athlete, and our training sessions often bordered on race effort because of the temperament he brought to practice combined with our individual talent levels. We all gain confidence from workouts, some of us by hitting certain times relative to the workout goals and others by how we measure up against training partners. I was motivated by the former, while Adam seemed more typically motivated by the latter.

Adam was an example of a runner who was able to maintain a high level of intensity and focus every single day, both for workouts and for races. For me, maintaining that intense level of competitive drive in practice and still being able to call on the necessary drive on race day would not have worked, but Adam seemed to have an endless supply of intensity from day to day.

For hard workouts, my style was very workmanlike. I tried to stay on an even keel and exert as little emotional energy as possible. I didn't pay attention to where I finished in a particular rep during a workout, just so long as I was meeting

continued >

the workout criteria. In some ways, that made Adam and me polar opposites. Despite that, we were good training partners, finding ways to make it work and complementing each other's abilities and temperaments.

Adam's requirement to stay a step ahead in practice was a part of his overall talent package; he was merely being true to his makeup, and it worked well for him. He was a hugely talented runner who excelled both in cross country (sixth at the 2006 world championships) and on the track (eighth at the 2007 world championships in the 5,000 and a 13:10 PR in that event). His unique ability to push himself on his own was one of his strong suits, and he trained very effectively alone. I was one of his few consistent training partners over the first part of his career; good training partners seemed to frustrate him more than they helped push him to a higher level of training. He did not need anyone else in order to push hard.

I enjoyed training with Adam. His intensity in practice was a large contributor to my success in racing because he elevated the productivity of workouts for me. And I am not knocking Adam's training approach because that was how he operated best, and he proved decisively that he could maintain an ongoing high level of intensity from day to day. He was a great runner. His weak link was not his ability to stay focused and continue to elevate his performance on race day but rather his body's ability to hold up over time.

The key to successful running with a training partner or a group is to remain true to your own talent package, temperament, motivation, current fitness level, and workout goals. Varying your effort, intensity, or emotional energy expenditure can have ill effects if such variations are not in line with who you are as an athlete.

or don't push hard enough when it is appropriate. You don't have to test your physical limits on a regular basis to know your individual threshold, nor do I recommend it. Hard training sessions can provide mixed feedback on your current state of fitness, depending on how rested you are and where you are in your development. Because it is so draining and doesn't provide the same definitive quantitative results as a race situation, frequently running hard in practice can lead to disappointment, frustration, and self-doubt. You can achieve insight into your thresholds simply by approaching your training with maturity, moderation, and self-awareness. You have to remove your ego and learn to turn off your competitiveness to some extent—not completely but just slightly.

There is a difference between the competitiveness required on race day and that utilized in training. While runners differ on the scale of competitive drive, all must show a level of restraint during training so as not to go over the edge. If you are the type who finds yourself getting way too aggressive and competitive over, say, a casual game of Ping-Pong or pool or bowling, then you may need to keep a close eye on your intensity when it comes to running.

Competitiveness is a very useful tool provided you use it to your advantage and do not let it become a distraction from your daily workout goals or your ultimate goals for the season. I let my competitiveness get the best of me on that run with Pat Porter. We often let our natural inclinations take over when we are out there running, and in particular when we are running hard. I am all about training hard and consider it a prerequisite to achievement, but it has to be tempered by smart training principles and balanced over the course of an entire training cycle.

Too Hard or Not Hard Enough?

Properly executing bouts of hard training is an art form; there is no definitive formula. Aside from understanding the prescribed workout and its intent, you must listen to your body, trust your judgment, and be mindful of the circumstances. Don't let competitiveness or a desire to prove something undermine the ultimate goal of furthering your training and providing the proper platform for actually racing well when it counts. Below are some of the areas in which discernment about effort and intensity is especially required.

Beware of Racing in Practice

Often in hard group workouts, one or more runners feels the need to substantiate the session by pushing a little harder to stay with the leaders or prove his or her worth. Or you might find yourself pushing to keep up with the group or an individual against whom you commonly measure yourself. Competitiveness has many upsides; however, it can have negative side effects in practice.

People react differently when faced with a competitive situation during a workout. Maybe you hate to lose. I understand that sentiment, believe me. However, competitiveness in training should be wielded in such a way that it benefits rather than weakens you. Keeping emotions in check during practice allows for consistent and effective workouts and also teaches you how to control (and appropriately unleash) that competitiveness in races.

Having a bit of competitive drive or a spark of energetic motivation in practice can help you push yourself to achieve the intended results of the workout. The challenge relates to pushing harder than you should. Every workout should have a specific purpose, and if a session is designed for a particular stimulus, then it must include the appropriate effort. Not utilizing the right effort not only negates the purpose and positive training effects of the workout but can also lead to the negative effects of excessive fatigue, overtraining, and overuse injuries and even lessen your race-day skills and instincts.

Some individuals allow competition in training to displace the race itself. For them, there is a decided sense of accomplishment in beating their training partners—perhaps an even more satisfying one than a PR or podium spot on race day.

Make sure that your confidence is not built on how you measure up against other individuals in your workout group. This attitude will ultimately limit your potential. While it is certainly appropriate to gauge your effort based on those around you and have a measure of competition to elevate the workout, your intensity cannot be based solely on your peers during practice. Develop instead an internal sense of what a hard effort should feel like tempered with a calm maturity that allows you to control your efforts.

Repeated competition in practice can also dilute the significance of racing itself and the ability to call on the emotional reserves needed to elevate a performance on race day. We only have a finite amount in the tank, and we constantly have to ration the output. Work, family, and other aspects of everyday life are all part of that equation as well. The goal is to make training as sustainable as possible so that you can draw on all the emotional reserves you need on race day.

Beware of Holding Back

The antithesis of being overly competitive in training sessions and lacking maturity when it comes to a healthy balance of competition in practice is holding back for the sake of the group. There are some athletes who don't want to cause hurt feelings or contention in the group dynamic.

Seeking out a group or an individual who complements your level is critical. Training with people who are below your level will eventually lead to slow or stagnating progress. The occasional easy day or easier-than-desired long run is fine within the scope of a three- to five-month training cycle. However, continually holding back for the sake of the group or friends or consistent training partners can lead to running below your potential.

> *You can achieve insight into your thresholds simply by approaching your training with maturity, moderation, and self-awareness.*

Most of my long runs were done with one or two individuals who complemented my ability and temperament. Scott Larson was my go-to training partner when it came to long runs because we had both undergone Coach Wetmore's tutelage and developed a healthy respect for the long run while not pushing it to the next level of intensity. Only rarely did I run with a large group for a long run, primarily because it almost always created a strained dynamic due to the fact that the runners were coming from various training programs, different coaching philosophies, and different points in their training cycles.

No matter what my focus or what I wanted to achieve from a long run, when all of those factors converged in a group long run, I was bound to have to compromise my goals. Group workouts can lead to ambiguous, unpredictable, or inconsistent efforts because there is often no collective goal. And even if there is a stated pacing goal for a long run, the various talent levels, personalities, and levels of fitness can skew that intent.

That was what happened during one particular group long run that I recall in Boulder. A group of guys all training at a high level met at the standard long-run location at the Boulder Reservoir. The intent was to run 18 to 20 miles, although no one had talked about how fast any of us really intended to run. Among the group of 15 or so runners were Larson, Mark Coogan, Pete Julian, and Marc Davis, all among the best in the country in events ranging from the 5K to the marathon. We started that run very conservatively and got to the first mile mark in about 8 minutes. Half jokingly Coogan said, "I think I actually lost fitness from that mile."

I was screaming inside to get going, but I did not want to appear to be the one trying to one-up everyone or start pushing the pace. For focused athletes with specific effort goals in mind, that can create an internal tension. I knew I had to decide to either do what I knew I needed to do or hold back for the sake of the group's ambiguous pacing. After a few not-so-subtle cues, Larson and I started to separate ourselves. Out of respect for the other runners, I mentioned that we were going to pick it up a bit, and it went over fine.

No matter what level of runner you are, the key is being honest with and respectful of your training partners. You need to stick to goals that are based on your training focus and where you are in your training cycle and not let the ambiguous intent of a group guide your workouts.

Beware of a Generic Approach

Every training program should include some uniquely tailored aspects to address your ability, specific goals, and overall physiology. We all have a unique combination of attributes, and therefore a unique approach is required for every athlete. A certain level of generalities is appropriate when abilities and goals overlap, but avoid lapsing into a generic approach that does not line up with your personal goals or ability. It is common for training groups to fall into the mode of everyone doing the same workout and the idea that as long as we are working hard, that is close enough. That approach is fine if you are new to the sport or just trying to get back to some semblance of fitness, but if you have a targeted goal, then an approach of "just getting out there a few days a week and doing a few hard sessions" won't cut it. A 3:45 marathoner should not be doing the same workout as a 3:15 marathoner, and a 45-minute 10K runner has different requirements than does a 35-minute 10K runner.

If sessions all start to fall into the same generic zone, then no one in the group will benefit as much as they could. Be sure that your training program and your group complement your goals; do not limit yourself by adopting the convenient option. It may require a touch more assertiveness on your part to help define the group, but it will be worth it on race day. This is not a matter of conceit or entitlement; it is critical to ensure that your efforts line up with your ability.

If you have trained with the same group over the years and fallen into a pattern of generically based workouts that don't line up with your ability or goal, it is time to step back, perhaps not to abandon the group altogether but instead to use it to your advantage. You can join in those group workouts early in your program or while coming off a break. Another option is to train with the group, but do your own versions of the workouts or individualized variations of portions of them. Sometimes just meeting the group for the warm-up is enough to provide the support and camaraderie that are needed. You might be doing a workout of 6 × 800 meters, while the group might be running 5 × 1 mile. Just having other athletes working out at the same time in the same location can elevate your efforts.

Running with Perceived Effort: Monitoring Versus Obsessing

Running has seen a major transformation over the last decade with the advancement of body-monitoring devices and wearable technology. The technological advancements of this digital age have led to a new level of analysis of a runner's training data that wasn't possible previously.

Before GPS-integrated tracking devices, there was no easy way to monitor real-time pacing except measuring your runs and taking splits along the way, unless of course you were running on a track.

Running on the track was always the standard when it came to being able to monitor a workout and check progression, which was why old-school guys like my dad liked to drive down to the high school track and knock out 3 or 4 miles around the oval for no other reason than it allowed him to check his pace. Track workouts were the best measure of fitness progress because they allowed you to compare workouts during a particular training season and over time.

Avoid Overtraining

In 1995, I watched a young Kenyan runner named Josephat Machuka absolutely destroy a very good field and the course record of the Bolder Boulder 10K. Like many young Kenyans in the 1990s, he burst onto the elite running scene after some top finishes at junior world championship races. He won the Bolder Boulder that day at the ripe young age of 21 in an almost incomprehensible time of 27:52 on the less-than-flat road course at high altitude.

Later that summer, he ran in the IAAF World Championships in Gothenburg, Sweden, where his youthful exuberance would not allow him to resist going gangbusters and running 27:29 to win his preliminary heat by 6 seconds. Two days later, in the 10,000 final, instead of winning easily (or even challenging for the win), he wound up a disappointing fifth. He ran well for another year—placing fifth in the 10,000-meter run at the 1996 Olympics—but then fell off the face of the elite running world before he turned 23.

Was Machuka overtrained? Most likely. With economic prosperity a huge carrot dangling as an incentive for running faster, it is not uncommon to see young Kenyans put in unfathomable amounts of training in their late teens and early 20s and rise quickly in the ranks of elite runners only to fizzle out and disappear even more quickly.

At the front end of extended bouts of overtraining, young runners can experience a period during which the negative biological and physiological effects take a while to kick in. But because athletes in this category are too focused on hard efforts and increasing volume, they don't pay enough attention to recovery efforts; rest; and, in many cases, a proper

continued >

nutritional balance. In the short term, it seems as if they break the rules for a while and get away with it, but in the long term, it always catches up with them and has devastating effects. While faster performances are initially possible, the decline begins almost immediately thereafter with a lack of energy and motivation and often turns into insomnia, decreased appetite, changes in blood pressure, and even depression.

Overtraining is not a phenomenon reserved for young Kenyan athletes. Dozens of top U.S. runners have fallen prey to overtraining, rising quickly and then disappearing from the competitive scene altogether. American great Alberto Salazar includes himself in that category. Before he turned 25, he'd won the New York City Marathon three times as well as the Boston Marathon and several U.S. championship track and cross country races, plus he'd set U.S. track records for the 5,000 and 10,000. But he was known for racing often, training with high intensity, and continually upping his weekly mileage, going from an average of 120 to 180 miles per week and even topping out at 200 miles on several occasions. His disappointing 15th place in the 1984 Olympic marathon, just five days after his 26th birthday, was the last competitive effort of his career except for a comeback victory of sorts at the 56-mile Comrades Marathon in South Africa 10 years later.

Some well-known American high school and college coaches have been known to put their athletes in similar situations, having their charges train with dangerously high mileage volume or intensity for several years with amazing results, only to have those runners struggle to accomplish anything at the next level.

Runners who overtrain typically have a few very good results but don't experience extended success and often have short-lived careers. And overtraining isn't limited to elites; it's also worrisome for recreational runners enticed into doing more than they should in a short period—such as ramping up mileage too quickly or doing too many hard workouts during a particular training cycle. Recreational runners who are building up training for a marathon and also working long hours are especially prone to overtraining,

Overtraining leads to chronic fatigue, poor sleep patterns, and a rash of overuse injuries. It can also wreak havoc on a runner's immune system and lead to other long-term physiological changes in a runner's makeup. The bottom line is that there are no shortcuts to reaching your long-term running goals. Avoid impulses to increase your training, squeeze in extra workouts, or continually try to do more while sacrificing recovery, rest, proper diet, and sleep. Monitor yourself for signs of overtraining, which can creep up on you. If you're feeling sluggish or stale in your training despite being very fit or aren't resting or eating properly, you should back off training and return to more realistic workloads and a smartly executed periodization plan.

Before GPS devices, runners would also often run a standard loop on the roads once or twice a week to check mile splits for a tempo run. The loop was measured by car, and all the mile markers were marked by some element such as a random tree or fire hydrant or an intersection with a cross street. When I was a young teen, I had my dad drive one of my standard runs from our house so I would know exactly where the mile splits were. In college, we knew where the mile splits were because their locations were handed down by upperclassmen. I encourage you too to go out and drive the course of your standard runs and familiarize yourself with where the mile markers are so that you can continually gauge your perceived effort and fitness. A GPS device will give you some of that feedback intermittently, but because the data and feedback are not immediate, it is harder to gauge a run or workout when relying on technology.

When you have accountability in your mile pace, you inevitably raise the effort level to ensure that the time reflected for that mile makes you feel good about the run. It also allows you to monitor your pacing as it relates to effort several days a week and then to simply run by feel on other days. Once it was impractical to monitor every single run day in, day out. But with the advent of technology, these fluctuations and variations from day to day, balanced by simply running by feel, have been all but eliminated. In recent years, many runners have monitored every mile—or even every few minutes—of every run. The obsession with immediate data derived from technology has eroded the skill of running by feel and the balance it provides.

In contrast, some athletes do not monitor their pacing at all, and their runs are all based on effort. Track workouts or measured loops are almost nonexistent, and every run is based on feel. Both the hyper-technological approach and the effort-as-the-only-measure approach have their merits and can prove extremely valuable when used properly, but the challenge comes with finding the right balance between them.

My wife always had a propensity to run too easy for her easy days, long runs, and tempo runs. Her track workouts were not an issue, but if given the option for her other sessions, she would tend to run on the low end of the spectrum and not take full advantage of the aerobic benefits that a daily run, long run, or tempo run could provide. She started monitoring her heart rate once she was able to fully understand where she needed to be depending on the effort.

Because it's not entirely accurate and it varies from runner to runner, heart rate training is tricky. My own heart rate zones fell within the standard formulas, so it was easy for me to use this tool. However, Shayne had a max heart rate of 215, and her zones were much higher and smaller than those of the typical athlete. It wasn't until she took a VO$_2$max treadmill test—an effort that shows the maximal point of maximal oxygen uptake and thus the top end of a runner's highest heart rate training zone—that she was able to fully understand how her heart rate should be implemented into her training. Later in her career, she used a GPS device to monitor her daily pace and, complementing these runs with track workouts, found the right balance of getting the information she needed to gain confidence and also gauge progression.

That said, she did listen to how she felt, and at least once or twice a week, she would trust how she felt regardless of what the heart rate monitor or GPS was telling her. There are always days when you don't feel great and should run slower regardless of what a device is telling you.

Monitoring heart rate is a way to get a better handle on how each day should feel—as long as you have a clear picture of your heart rate zones. The zones are not universal, and heart rate is affected by numerous variables—including hydration, caffeine, sleep, illness, and fatigue—so it is far from foolproof. It can be a good guide, but there are always exceptions, and even with close monitoring, heart rate must be accompanied by acute self-awareness.

When I was training very hard and running 115 to 120 miles per week, I struggled to get my heart rate up. I was carrying so much fatigue that my heart rate would be 6 to 8 beats per minute lower than it should be for a tempo run, for instance. Even if I had wanted to get my heart rate up higher for those workouts, I would have defeated the purpose and in effect would have run too hard. Effort is relative to where you are in a training cycle. During a tapering period, you can run quicker for easy days because you are running so much less overall volume. If your heart rate is a few beats higher for your easy days, that's fine because you will still be able to recover appropriately due to running less volume.

I did not need a GPS watch or heart rate monitor to make me push harder on my long runs or easy days. I used a heart rate monitor to ensure that I was in the correct zone for tempo runs and some harder runs above threshold, but more often than not what the monitor told me did not affect how fast or slow I ran that day. Having trained for the majority of my career via measured runs and track sessions, I was always keenly aware of effort and pacing.

There is no one way to approach learning the skill of perceived effort, but daily monitoring via GPS or a complete lack of any measure and just running how you feel every day do not lend to learning this skill. You need to find a happy medium. It comes from months of monitoring runs and workouts with consistency and developing an internal sense of what your effort feels like and then being disciplined and discerning enough to scale back the monitoring from time to time. No matter whether you use a high-tech electronic device or figure out your pace with an old-school digital watch, you need to understand how those efforts feel so they become instinctual. On race day, you want to be able to trust that sense of feel and ride the razor's edge of being neither lulled into a pace that's too slow nor lured into a pace that's too fast.

No world records have ever been set while wearing a GPS or heart rate monitor, and likewise no one winning a gold medal in the Olympics just runs how they feel every day without any measure of their pacing. You have to find the right balance for you. Some athletes require more consistent feedback to ensure that they stay accountable to the effort for that day, while others just need it occasionally to check in. Everyone needs to check their progress, and I strongly believe track sessions or measured loops are still the best options.

But it's very important to note that there is a difference between monitoring your training data and obsessing about it. It's OK to check your pacing during a run or even every 200 meters while running on the track, but looking at your watch every 8 seconds during a run is a dreadful habit that can only lead to mental and emotional challenges. The biggest problem is that it can lead to a lack of trust in what your body is telling you. You have to learn to trust how you feel, or your wearable technology devices will start to hold you back.

Champion performances come when runners trust the feedback their body is giving them and get their mind out of the way of what their body is capable of doing. That said, it's impossible to fully develop in your training if you do not have any accountability to your pace and fitness, and that requires checking in either by GPS, track workouts, or measured runs. Without some standard, you'll either be running slower than you think you are, running harder for a portion of a session but not the whole session, or running the whole session harder than is appropriate given the type of workout.

Perceived effort is becoming a lost art and must be practiced if there is any hope of running at your best on race day. Use a GPS or heart rate monitor some of the time; just don't forget to trust how you feel. If you obsess about your pace and the analytical data it provides or find yourself checking your watch incessantly, then stop using it every day. Bust out an old basic stopwatch and just run. However, if you haven't been gauging your efforts, then it's time to start.

– 5 –

TRAINING

PERIODIZATION

Now that we have sifted through the psychology of your motivation, talked about how to develop and maintain balance, and outlined some of the mental principles required, we can actually talk about training. Let's be honest: This is the good stuff, the meat and potatoes of what we do as runners. Racing may be the glamorous part, where you get a chance to put it all together and go for it, but training is what we do every day and what consumes our focus on the way to chasing those ultimate goals in the rare moments of racing. That's not to devalue or deemphasize the importance of racing, but ultimately training—and the continual efforts that go into it—is what makes us the runners we are.

The Long-Term Approach to Training

The objective of this chapter and the next one is to give an overview of the various necessary training elements as well as some variations in how to approach them. We have all heard that there is more than one way to skin a cat, or that there's more than one path to the top of a mountain. That is very much the case when it comes to training for a long-distance running race, primarily because we all have a unique physiological makeup. If we were all the same, then a one-size-fits-all, cookie-cutter approach to training would suffice for everybody. But it's important to understand that even though we might be doing the same things or have similar end goals, it's our physiological differences—and how we train based on those differences—that can have the biggest impact on our ability to progress as runners and ultimately reach those goals.

Ultimately training—and the continual efforts that go into it—is what makes us the runners we are.

For example, two runners might have similar athletic talent, similar backgrounds in running, and even similar PRs. But it's very likely they're still far more different than they are alike. Our ability to process oxygen efficiently, our maximum heart rate, heart rate at threshold, muscle makeup biopsy, and anaerobic buffering capabilities are all part of our individual blueprint, and each of those elements factors into our training protocol. Training under a plan that does not make individual adjustments to your training will not yield the best results. It is like making a cake without following a recipe and lacking the full set of necessary ingredients. You might still be able to whip something up, put it in the oven, cover it in frosting, and call it cake, but it is hit or miss whether it's going to be good or not. When it comes to running, that approach might mean that you finish your marathon 10 or 20 minutes slower than you had hoped or miss a 10K PR by less than a minute. The effort is still admirable, but it falls short of what you aimed for.

If you care about performance-oriented running goals, you need to understand some of the science behind training and put in the time and effort to follow specific steps of development. There are many common truths about the physiological aspects of training that have been tested and proven over time. If you dissect the training of the most accomplished runners, you will find that they follow similar principles that have been part of the core beliefs of the sport for more than 60 years. While many of those principles have evolved as runners, coaches, and physiologists continue to push the envelope with smart individual adaptations, the essential ideas have remained mostly unchanged. The key to smart training is understanding how to apply those principles on an individual basis. That's why training the body and the mind for long-distance running is very much both a science and an art.

Of course there are always a few exceptions to the rule, the runners who seem to do everything wrong and still see a high level of success. Supremely gifted runners can break some of the rules, and you might know runners in your local running circles who do it too. Talent and hard work can overcome a lot of things—including inconsistency, common sense, and the application of trusted protocols. But that kind of training method will not work on a long-term basis. Few runners can get away with an off-the-grid or inconsistent training regimen and achieve success regularly or predictably. Runners who run hard all the time are prone to overtraining. Runners who don't properly build a base or hone their speed or execute long intervals might turn in a few good workouts or races, but they typically come up short over the scope of an entire season.

The focus here is not on a short-term approach to training. It is all too common to overtrain by running too hard every day or running a significant session before periodized training has built up the body's natural ability to absorb the training. Don't get lured into that approach. If you have already, then you have likely suffered from ongoing frustration because you don't understand why you can't get back to those levels and seem to never feel good or comfortable while training or racing.

Running like a champion involves a long-term approach aimed at foreseeable results balanced against reasonable expectations. Let me be frank: There is no way around hard training if you want to reach

Running like a champion involves a long-term approach aimed at foreseeable results balanced against reasonable expectations.

your ultimate running goals. Everyone has a threshold depending on physiological makeup, history, number of years running, age, and susceptibility to injury, but no matter how your personal deck is stacked, consistent hard work is required. As we discussed earlier in the book, you cannot finesse your way to a significant goal or waver in your consistency or dedication. There are no gimmicks or magical workouts for improving as a runner. Sound, productive training means following the correct methods and principles. It will sometimes be difficult. Days or even weeks of feeling fatigued should be expected and not avoided. There are times when a feeling of overall fatigue is good; it means you are pushing your body to adjust to a new level of fitness. But as with every aspect of training, it comes down to balance and finding that place where you know you are tired but the quality of the training is not suffering. The Olympic approach includes regimented, solid training; making the most of your efforts; and doing as much as you can with the time available to you.

Maybe in the past you have followed generic programs and felt as though you were just spinning your wheels. Perhaps you were getting some nuance of your training wrong: too many or too few cumulative miles, running hard on easy days or vice versa, or arranging the phases of your training in a counterproductive way. Whatever the reason, do not despair. Your running goals are very much within reach if you follow the approach laid out in this book.

Be open to thinking differently and trying something new. I have spent my career speaking with athletes, reading, observing, listening to my body, and trying new things to get the right balance. There is not one prescription to fit everyone. Ultimately it is up to you to take ownership and be willing to pay attention to what is working or not working as you go through the process, adapting and experimenting to find out what works best for you. The training you need to do is specific to who you are, how you feel on a daily and weekly basis, and everything else that's going on in your life.

The training elements and the principles behind them discussed in this chapter and the next one can be applied to any program. The more specific the goal or the further you progress in your overall development, the more individualized your approach should be. But by and large, if you train with intention, you will see the desired improvement and, ultimately, position yourself to reach your goals.

Periodization

Periodization is an organizing system that breaks down your training into periods or cycles that fit into an overall macrocycle for a particular season. Most Olympic-level runners follow some type of periodization plan because it is a proven method for achieving consistent results across numerous years. As popular and proven as the system is among elite athletes, most running enthusiasts do not apply it. Why? For some, it is a challenge to commit to a long-term approach. For others, it comes down to a lack of consistency. Some don't fully understand the benefits. The most common approach by the enthusiast is to jump headlong into training and hope for a bump in fitness and improvement in performance through week after week of hard workouts. That approach may temporarily produce good results, but those results are usually limited, unpredictable, and short-term.

I call this condition "false fitness," a tenuous level of fitness that is earned quickly following a haphazard, intense period of training and crumbles easily if circumstances arise that interrupt training due to illness, injury, life issues, or long breaks between training periods. Those runners tend to duplicate the same kind of training program year after year, and while they seem to get into better shape rather rapidly, they never make a significant step forward.

The key to periodization is committing to the various cycles built into a plan over a full year with every workout element intentionally and strategically placed within that system. The time frame can be shortened to accommodate a specific goal race, but 12 months is ideal, as it typically coincides with the various racing seasons in a calendar year. A training program haphazardly built on random workouts executed as you feel like it or can make time will ultimately allow for only a moderate level of improvement. You cannot rely on unpredictable or inconsistent mileage, inconsistent long runs, and random "down" periods or frequent missed workouts to be building blocks for your development. The best way to reach your goals as a distance runner is to adhere to the structure of periodization that has been proven through time.

So what does periodization actually look like? How many cycles are there, and how long should each be? What kind of workouts should be included in each cycle?

The Base Phase

The Base Phase, while not easy, is the most straightforward of all the phases. It is easier to execute because the emphasis is primarily on mileage consistency of the weekly long run and various types of aerobic training. In other words, there is more margin for error. (Other phases require more precision and a wider variety of workouts in order to achieve the desired race results.) The Base Phase lasts for 12 to 18 weeks and is arguably the most important part of the year because it lays the foundation and allows for a quantifiable increase in aerobic fitness, which will set you up for success when your training moves on to the next phases. The early weeks of the Base Phase are especially key because that is when the largest gains may be made. However, if you do not have a decent level of fitness going into this

Physiological Training Systems

The body adapts to exercise in myriad ways during a properly executed training periodization plan. These time-tested physiological training systems are engaged in a periodized plan in order to train the body's ability to use oxygen to create energy for your muscles under running and racing conditions that include various levels of fatigue. Think of building your aerobic fitness like building a house. To build a house, you need a solid foundation before you can put up walls, install doors, and hang cabinets. Then you need paint and flooring before you can decorate with art, lighting, or other final touches. To train your body for long-distance running, you need a foundation of aerobic fitness in order to develop greater fitness with higher levels of training and ultimately fine-tune your body for racing. The key to periodization is to continually reinforce that foundation while smartly implementing other types of training.

Aerobic Training

Aerobic training is the type of running you do when it is easy to process oxygen efficiently. Although many people equate it only with running at slow to moderate paces, aerobic training has a broad range, from slow recovery paces and moderate long-run paces all the way to longer-distance race paces (including marathon pace). An aerobic training pace is a pace you can seemingly hold indefinitely without feeling like you're breathing too hard. Aerobic running passes the "talk test," which means you're able to speak in complete sentences to running partners. (At the faster paces described below, talking is more difficult and often limited to short phrases or incomplete thoughts.) Simply put, during aerobic running,

continued >

your body is able to use all of the oxygen it needs to produce the energy your muscles need to perform. Most of the running you do each week falls into the aerobic category, especially recovery runs, portions of the long run, and warm-up and cooldown sessions before and after harder workouts.

Lactate Threshold Training

Lactate threshold training is the type of running you do on the edge of your ability to process oxygen efficiently. Your lactate threshold is your aerobic threshold—the fastest pace you can run without having your body produce more lactic acid than your body can utilize and convert into energy. As a result, the lactic acid begins to accumulate in the bloodstream and makes it moderately harder to run. Lactate threshold training is typically associated with runs that are "comfortably hard," often at a pace close to a 10-mile or half-marathon race pace. It's hard but not so hard that you can't sustain the pace for a long time (at least 70 to 90 minutes for well-trained runners). The effort should feel within your capability but uncomfortable, and you should not be able to have a conversation aside from sharing a few words at a time. The most common types of lactate threshold training are tempo runs and fartlek runs, or tempo intervals. Tempo runs are typically sustained efforts of 20 to 60 minutes at a pace that puts you in (or close to) a state of slight discomfort, and fartlek runs, or tempo intervals, are runs that include similar hard tempo-paced running for intermittent periods. Periodization training will allow you to get stronger over time and improve your lactate threshold (by lowering the pace at which your body starts to produce more lactic acid than it can process) so you can run faster and more efficiently with less effort.

Anaerobic Threshold Training

Anaerobic means "without oxygen," and your anaerobic threshold is the point at which your body can no longer efficiently process oxygen, resulting in lactic acid building up in the bloodstream faster than your body is able to remove it. Running at a pace that is right at your threshold feels very hard and is difficult to sustain for long—typically 12 to 25 minutes at a time. Good examples of anaerobic training are long intervals run at 5K, 10K, or 15K race pace. Anaerobic threshold training teaches your system to buffer the effects of lactic acid longer and also to use the lactate as fuel. Ultimately, an increased anaerobic threshold will allow you to race at a faster pace over long distances without fatigue becoming overwhelming.

Anaerobic Training

Anaerobic training is the type of running you do when you do not have sufficient oxygen to produce the energy your muscles need. It is very hard and cannot be sustained for long—typically less than a minute for most runners. Short sprint intervals are the only real form of anaerobic training, and you might also find yourself running anaerobically during an all-out sprint to the finish line of a race. Anaerobic training is important in building top-end speed and fine-tuning the upper reaches of your cardiovascular strength, ultimately allowing your body to run as effectively as possible at high speeds despite being extremely fatigued.

phase, it is also where you might feel the most sore, fatigued, and exasperated. The body takes time to adjust to any sudden increase in mileage; therefore, it is advisable to be at least relatively fit before beginning. Every Olympic-caliber runner takes time off after a racing season, but they then spend weeks re-creating a solid foundation of basic fitness before launching into the Base Phase of their training cycle. That initial fitness, which comes from moderate mileage at moderate paces, is the buildup phase that leads into the Base Phase. Starting a Base Phase "off the couch" or ramping up mileage from a low amount to a significantly higher amount can be tiresome, debilitating, and dangerous.

Benefits of the Base Phase

Of the many significant benefits of a Base Phase, aerobic conditioning is the most notable. Continual consistent running for several months with a focus on higher mileage, increased long-run duration, and longer workouts leads to an overall increase in aerobic enzymes, and that leads to the ability to process oxygen better for longer periods of time. While there are many ways you can train and many systems that you can improve, there is no substitute for consistent mileage. (For a detailed discussion on systems, see the "Physiological Training Systems" sidebar, page 103.) Coach Wetmore used to half-jokingly say that any athlete who wanted to try out for the University of Colorado cross country team should "run 100 miles a week for the next year and then come back and see me." Most runners don't prefer this type of training, so it was one way of testing their resiliency. But his main point was that a good base of training was the most effective and simple way to improve. Without that high level of aerobic fitness, a runner couldn't (and shouldn't) attempt to engage in next-level workouts because it would be too much of a struggle without the foundation for progress. It would be like asking elementary school students to attempt calculus equations when their highest level of math involved multiplication tables and long division or like asking a high school student on the debate team to serve as a public defender in a major court case. The bottom line is that you need to first build a solid foundation in order to progress as a runner.

Elite athletes usually hit their athletic peak after many years of high-level training. This is primarily due to having a Base Phase year after year and thus developing a higher cumulative aerobic capacity. Speed is developed relatively quickly, as is the body's ability to buffer lactic acid. However, gaining substantial amounts of oxygen-carrying enzymes at the cellular level takes the most time, and this gain is achieved via a solid Base Phase. Greater oxygen-carrying capacity means you not only have the ability to race at a higher level but can also maintain a higher level of fitness and remain in peak racing fitness for an extended period. That is why a high-level track runner can race consistently from midspring until the end of summer and why a road racer can often race a variety of short- to long-distance races during a summer-and-fall season.

You can get marginally prepared for a race with the false fitness I referred to earlier. But that kind of fitness is based on 11th-hour race-readiness, not true overall comprehensive conditioning. It allows for only a small margin of error in training, and if that runner becomes sick or suffers a minor injury, he or she tends to lose fitness rapidly. If that's been your approach in the past, you may find that you easily get overly fatigued from training, which leads to unwanted results, not only physically but also psychologically. You become more susceptible to illness, your sleep patterns become irregular, and you can't develop a balanced perspective about your training and fitness because your physical condition wavers back and forth.

In contrast, there is no greater feeling for a runner than going into a racing season knowing you are strong. You can feel it in everything you do, and it all starts with a properly administered Base Phase. A well-built base not only serves as the foundation for your season of racing—a platform on which you will continue to build your fitness with additional workouts—but it also gives you confidence and reinforced enthusiasm to keep working toward your goals. It also allows you to maintain your fitness longer through a given racing season.

The Base Phase begins with a four-week window of primarily running easy and building your overall mileage to the highest weekly mileage you have achieved in the previous two to three years. For example, if your highest weekly total in previous years was 60 miles per week, you should aim to gradually progress to that goal by the fourth week of your Base Phase. To get there, your weekly long run should gradually increase and should be more of a moderate effort than an easy-day effort. During this first part of the Base Phase, building overall volume is the primary emphasis, and you should aim to increase mileage by roughly 20 percent each week. Although no specific workouts should be performed during this first four weeks, you should include some small doses of intensity with a few fast strides (5K race-pace repeats for 10 to 20 seconds but not all-out sprints) after an easy run and one or two days a week of more moderate effort.

The next six weeks of the Base Phase should include an increase in mileage by roughly 10 percent each week and a 15 percent increase in the long run each week. To avoid feeling stale, plan for a "down" week after three weeks to allow your body a bit of recovery amid your buildup. A down week is not an off week but rather a week during which you run the mileage comparable to four weeks earlier—so roughly about 20 percent less than your maximum-mileage week. This adjustment is critical during the Base Phase; otherwise cumulative fatigue will set in, and training will start to suffer. Fatigue is a natural part of training and is not to be completely avoided, but when it causes workout quality to suffer, then the training is not being fully absorbed. (For older athletes, a down week might be necessary every two weeks.)

Also included during this six-week period should be one faster workout per week. Workouts should be fartlek in nature: short intervals (45 to 90 seconds) with longer recovery periods between reps, hill

Strides

Strides, also called buildups, wind sprints, or striders, are an effective tool used to acclimate the body to fast running, build neuromuscular timing, and instill good running form. Strides are essentially a series of short, fast-paced efforts of 10 to 20 seconds at a pace that falls somewhere between your fastest mile pace and your fastest 5K pace. They are meant to be not all-out sprints but instead short bouts of quick running with a hint of intensity. The recovery interval between each should be about 30 seconds to 1 minute of easy jogging or walking.

When doing strides, focus on good form (upright posture with a slight lean, full leg extension, good powerful toe-off from the ground, a compact and controlled arm swing, and a stable head) without overstriding or exerting too much muscular force.

Buildup strides are a variation that entails running a more moderate, controlled pace at the start and finish of a stride with faster-paced running in the middle. For example, in a 20-second stride, that might mean running for 5 seconds at 70 to 75 percent effort, followed by 10 seconds at 80 to 85 percent effort, followed by 5 seconds at 70 to 75 percent effort.

It's a good idea to do some light stretching after strides to keep the leg muscles loose.

repeats (30 to 60 seconds), longer intervals (4 to 8 minutes), or tempo runs. Rotate the workouts each week to touch on all the various systems. The focus is still on overall mileage and the moderate-effort long run, but now you can add the faster workout into the mix.

The last period of four to six weeks should include an additional workout in your weekly routine. Any of the workout types mentioned above are ideal, with one to two easy days between them. Weekly mileage and long-run distance should not increase during this period. And again, another down week should be factored in after two to three weeks. The additional workout added into the week will complement the adaptation to the mileage and the long run.

Speed, Pacing, and Volume in the Base Phase

Along with some longer interval workouts (something with intervals in the 3- to 8-minute range, such as mile repeats on the track) and tempo efforts, speed work should be a part of your Base Phase workouts (albeit not in the early weeks). The difference between Base Phase speed workouts and those later in the season is the amount of rest between intervals. During the Base Phase, you should take more rest during speed sessions, with a focus on hitting the designated times rather than on forcing the recovery. This is a great time to run hills or shorter interval track workouts such as 400s—but again, with lots of recovery. Getting fast while still primarily developing your overall aerobic strength will pay off. For one, your everyday pace benefits from some speed training, and so do your other workouts. How so? Your nervous-system development and fast-twitch fiber development allow for greater speed transfer in longer-interval or tempo workouts.

Efficiency, power, and turnover should always be included during speed workouts, and focusing only on longer speed workouts is a mistake. Bob Kennedy, former American-record holder in the 3K and 5K on the track and the first non-African to break 13 minutes for the 5K, once shared his insights on workouts in his Base Phase. He said that even during his Base Phase, when he was running heavy volume—130 to 140 miles a week at times—he would still go to the track and run 400s in under 60 seconds every 10 days. Later in the season, when his fitness was more fine-tuned, he would run those 400s in 57 seconds with shorter recovery.

Because the vast majority of the Base Phase is made up of easy runs, a focus on everyday pace is important. It is tempting to run very slowly on easy runs since you are running more volume overall. However, once you are through the initial buildup period and have adapted to the higher volume of work, then easy-day pace should be adjusted slightly. Throughout a training cycle, your everyday pace should always fall into the range of comfortable, moderate-paced running, but it will naturally get quicker in the Transition Phase and Race Phase. The key is to run as quickly as you can while still recovering, not to run as slowly as you need to recover.

Workout volume should also be considered. As mentioned, this is the time of year to include longer but slightly less intense workouts. Also, more rest between intervals is appropriate to compensate for the added fatigue carried in the legs. You can't always perform at a high level, and something always has to give. What should give during this phase is rest between intervals and overall intensity of intervals. What should not be compromised are total volume, long-run length, and easy-day pace.

You should finish your Base Phase feeling notably stronger mentally and physically. And because you have increased your ability to process oxygen and improved your lactate threshold, you should experience an increase in your tempo pace at the same relative effort. In other words, you can run more efficiently and faster for the same distance at the same level of output. Bigger mileage volume weeks toward the end of the cycle should be more manageable and less exhausting. Certainly you might feel short stretches of fatigue from the increased workload—which is why you need to be sure to get enough sleep and stay sufficiently hydrated—but you should not feel overly fatigued or beaten down. Instead, your increased aerobic base should have you feeling more energized and powerful.

The Transition Phase

The Transition Phase is just that: the transition from the volume- and strength-focused Base Phase to a period with more race-specific workouts. The main goal of this phase is to prepare the body for the intensity that will come with racing, and it is also the period during which the nervous system gets called into action to get race pace dialed in as well. Overall volume should remain on the high side but with a greater focus on more-intense workouts with shorter recovery between intervals, pacing that is closer to goal race pace, and a (slightly) shorter weekly long run. If done properly, the strength you bring from the Base Phase will facilitate this shift to more intense workouts in the Transition Phase. Easy to moderate running on the days between workouts is very important for the body to be able to recover and adapt.

The Transition Phase is four to eight weeks in duration. The first four weeks should still include high-volume weeks (initially equivalent to the peak of the Base Phase) and longer long runs; however, a gradual decrease in volume over the last two to four weeks is necessary to accommodate the more intense workouts in this phase. Some weeks during the first month of the Transition Phase will still need to be very close to the maximum mileage of the Base Phase, but that volume needs to be balanced with more variation from week to week. If harder workouts are included in a given week, then a reduction in mileage (up to 10 percent) should also be included.

Your long run during this phase should include greater variation as well. Vary the run by 4 to 8 miles, depending on other workouts during a particular week. If you are coming off a week that included workouts with shorter intervals and more recovery, for example, then a higher-volume week with a longer long run is in order. In contrast, if your week included a longer interval workout and longer tempo run, then a shorter long run is appropriate along with cutting back a few miles on your recovery runs.

Buildup races are another key element of the Transition Phase. Buildup races are meant to create a greater bump in fitness due to the race intensity and to get your mind and body used to the discomfort that comes with racing. Although these races should be taken seriously, they should be considered a training element. Positive results are possible if a proper Base Phase was implemented, but don't expect to set a PR or even race to your fullest potential. Your focus is on gaining more fitness from these events. Races during this phase are a great way to practice race pace for a longer race in a shorter distance, for example, running a 10K at your goal half-marathon pace or running a half-marathon at the end of a solid week of mileage at marathon goal pace. Another element to consider for buildup races is under-distance racing. If you are training to run a half- or full marathon, this is an optimal time to run a 5K and 10K event. The key to these races is to not be fully tapered, rested, and fresh; otherwise you start to sacrifice your ability to maintain all the added aerobic strength that accompanied the Base Phase. (Tapering and going into races really fresh needs to be saved for later in the process, when you're running target races tied to your ultimate goals.) Avoid racing too often during this phase—racing once a month is a good rule of thumb. Otherwise you'll start to compromise too many weeks of training and chip away at the competitive edge you will need as you close in on your primary goal.

The Race Phase

The Race Phase represents the culmination of your training and sharpens the focus on your target races and ultimate goals. It is also a phase during which many enthusiast runners struggle, not because they don't enjoy racing but because their training has often been too general to allow for a proper peak. Ideally, individuals lay out the year and include a race every few months. That time frame should include a Base Phase with no races, a Transition Phase with some tune-up events that are focused on gaining fitness, and ultimately a period—the Race Phase—with multiple races during which you are working toward peak fitness for the year.

Ideally, the Race Phase is a four- to six-week window with several races. If you have a strong level of fitness, it's OK to do four to six shorter races (5K to 10K) during this period, but I would recommend doing only three longer races (10 miles to 25K) during a six-week Race Phase. For shorter races up to the half-marathon, executing a handful of buildup races during the Race Phase is key, as is a shift in workouts to allow the body to be ready for an all-out race effort.

It is important to note that this principle does not apply to the marathon. Buildup races are not as critical for the marathon and can actually be detrimental in the six-week crescendo that leads up to the race date. Rather, the pre-race taper is the biggest factor in optimal peaking for that event. A proper taper executed in the final 10 days to 3 weeks of a marathon racing phase should entail a gradual reduction in mileage each week and lessening the frequency and duration of harder workout sessions. I typically reduced my mileage by about 25 percent 3 weeks out, another 15 percent with 2 weeks to go, and then another 10 percent in the week leading up to a marathon. I would still do faster workouts during my taper, but I would reduce the number of reps and not do those workouts as often. The goal of a marathon taper is to reduce your level of muscular fatigue while keeping your engine revving and ready to race. You don't want to go cold turkey and start relaxing—that would be disastrous come race day because your body will be less able to respond to the intensity of your race pace. On the contrary, a good taper period should maintain a bit of intensity while avoid beating you up with the sustained harder efforts you experienced during the Transition Phase and first part of the Race Phase.

The more volume you run during the bulk of your training, the more aggressive the tapering should be. The percentages listed above do not equate exactly if you run less volume. For instance, if you max

Training Phases

Here is a quick breakdown of the phases of a training cycle with some insight into what kind of running and what to expect in each phase.

Buildup Phase

No matter what your previous level or experience of running, this initial phase of training will give you a better relative base of fitness and prepare you for the higher volume of running during the Base Phase. During this four- to eight-week phase, mileage will be moderate; the key is to get yourself physically fit and mentally focused for the challenges of a structured training plan with consistent efforts and commitments.

Base Phase

The Base Phase is the primary building block of your training program. You build aerobic strength during this 12- to 18-week phase through long runs, higher weekly mileage volume, and some basic types of harder workouts that will allow you to effectively do more advanced workouts and fine-tune your fitness in later phases. This period should not consist of only easier runs; you need to include a few aerobic, marathon-paced harder workouts. A good guideline would be to include one harder workout per week for weeks 1 to 6 and two harder workouts per week for weeks 6 to 10. While all phases are important, you can't skimp on the Base Phase because the rest of your training is predicated on having a solid aerobic foundation.

continued >

Transition Phase

The four- to eight-week Transition Phase of a training program enables your body to transition from a period of building volume and strength to a period focused on race-specific workouts. Mileage remains relatively high during this phase but gradually decreases to accommodate the increased intensity of workouts. You will touch on speed and more challenging efforts and will also start to reap the benefits of your Base Phase by feeling strong and fit.

Race Phase

The Race Phase is the final phase, the culmination period in which you fine-tune your fitness for racing and race several shorter-distance races or prepare for one final target marathon or similar long-distance goal event. Weekly mileage decreases from previous phases, but intensity is vastly increased to create race-day sharpness. You should feel fast, fit, and energized during this phase and mentally captivated by the possibility of reaching your long-term race goals.

Rest Phase

The Rest Phase is often overlooked by runners as an actual phase of a training program, but ensuring that you take time off and engage in active rest following the Race Phase is an important part of a runner's continuing progression. The length of the Rest Phase will vary depending on what kind of racing you did during the Race Phase and when you plan to begin your next training cycle. Taking time off with no running at all is key to this phase, as is running easy, running for fun, and running without a watch or any type of monitoring.

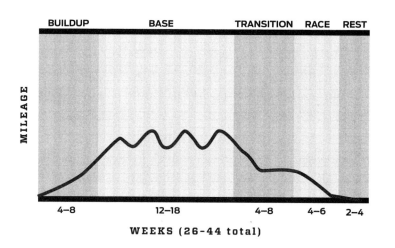

BUILDUP	BASE	TRANSITION	RACE	REST

MILEAGE

| 4–8 | 12–18 | 4–8 | 4–6 | 2–4 |

WEEKS (26-44 total)

out at 55 miles per week, then a reduction of 25 percent 3 weeks out is too aggressive. It should be closer to a 15 percent reduction at that point, followed by another 15 percent reduction 2 weeks out and 10 percent the week prior to your race.

Here are three things to consider during your taper.

- Don't slow down. Many people start both tapering back their mileage and running slower each day. This will lead to feeling flat and your legs feeling dead. If anything, your day-to-day pace can increase slightly since you are running less volume and will be able to recover more easily.
- Back off your mileage gradually rather than dramatically, and certainly not all at once right at the end. Dropping mileage too quickly will leave you feeling flat and awkward in the days before the race and on race day.
- Go with variety. Do not do only short, fast workouts just because they are short and sweet. Too much speed work in the final two

weeks will leave you fatigued with dead legs. Do a session or two of longer reps during your taper (maybe 4 × 1 mile or 4 × 1,000 at 5K race pace) and touch on tempo effort as well (with a shorter tempo run that is on the cusp of your half-marathon race pace). This will keep your body in tune with the training you've done all along.

Mileage is less of a focus during this phase. Think of your volume like a bell curve starting from the beginning of the buildup in the Base Phase, hitting its peak during the Base Phase and early in the Transition Phase and then coming back down during the Race Phase. Weekly volume at the start and end of that curve will be about 40 percent less than your maximum weeks. The higher the volume you run, the greater the fluctuation in overall mileage. For example, if you hit a maximum of 60 miles in a week during your Base Phase and early in the Transition Phase, then a 35- to 40-mile week is appropriate in the Race Phase.

The long run during the Race Phase should be considerably shorter than those in your Base Phase and Transition Phase. Essentially, it should entail adding a few miles to your longest easy run during this phase. For example, if you do 6 miles as your standard easy-day run, then a 10-mile run would be the longest distance you would need for a long run.

Workout intensity during the Race Phase should be higher, and recovery between intervals should be shorter. For instance, if you run 400-meter repeats with a 1:30 rest break during the Transition Phase, that workout should be adapted during the Race Phase so that fewer 400-meter repeats are executed but with a rest break reduced to about 1:00. Total volume of workouts should also go down to complement the greater intensity and reduced rest within workouts. Easy days should become a touch quicker to help maintain overall blood volume. Since total mileage is lower and the long run is shorter, increasing your pace by 10 to 20 seconds per mile is appropriate. That applies to both easy runs and your weekly long run, but it is more important to run slightly faster on easy days. Also, it is important to run strides two or three times a week following easy runs. Strides are 10- to 20-second sprints at 5K race pace effort (see the "Strides" sidebar). Shoot for doing six total, with the first two at about 70 percent effort, the next two at 80 percent effort, and the final two at 90 percent effort.

– 6 –

TRAINING

THE WORKOUTS

Now that we've explored the big picture of periodized training phases, we will zero in on the runs and workouts that make up those phases. The two keys in this chapter are understanding the essence of each type of run or workout, how they differ, and the importance of where each is placed in your weekly regimen. While each type of run has its own singular importance, remember that training for a long-term running goal is a comprehensive package of the runs and workouts you do combined with good recovery, nutrition, hydration, and sleep habits plus your mental outlook and how running fits into your life. While every run and workout plays a role in your development, no single run should be overemphasized or considered more important than another.

Long Runs

Over the last two decades, the long run has become more and more of an integral focus for the general population of runners. This was probably first prompted by a better understanding of the physiological benefits of the long run and the work by progressive thinkers such as notable coaches Arthur Lydiard and Joe Henderson. Following on their work, many other running coaches and authors have created programs with a central focus on the long run, and many runners looking to simply complete a marathon adopted an approach centered on the long run. The long run has been further popularized by running magazines and websites.

Certainly Olympic champions such as Frank Shorter and Joan Benoit Samuelson included the long run as an important part of their training; however, it was not the entire focus of their training. Unfortunately, there are misconceptions about the role the long run plays in an overall plan, and it is often either overemphasized or improperly executed. No doubt the long run is critical, but don't get lured into thinking it is the only ingredient necessary for success or that running longer just to increase your mileage will have huge payoffs. Indeed, just jogging along mile after mile may actually prevent you from reaching your goals.

The long run is the anchor of a training week, and other significant sessions should be planned around the timing of this key piece of training. However, the long run is but one element, not the entire focus, of a program. There are huge physiological benefits to consistently running properly timed and executed long runs, but without the complement of short and long intervals, fartlek and tempo runs—not to mention recovery runs and rest days—the long run becomes little more than mileage added to the week. It can—and should—be much more than that.

A long run every seven days is the most common standard for runners training for races ranging from 5K to the marathon. As a rule of thumb, the long run should not make up more than 35 percent of your total weekly volume. For example, if you run 50 miles a week, then a 20-mile long run (40 percent of that volume) is excessive. Something closer to 14 to 16 miles is more appropriate during the majority of your Base Phase and allows your body to recover for other important workout sessions throughout the week. It might be enticing to run an epic long run on the weekend, but if that is followed by three or four days of little to no running due to physical or mental fatigue, then minimal benefit has been gained. You are much better served by running a 10-mile long run as part of a week that includes five or six other days of running with one or two harder sessions.

When I was first introduced to hard, high-level training at the University of Colorado, the long run was the first element we explored. Although I had done long runs in high school, they had not been a major focus for me as a young athlete, nor had mileage volume. Speed work, easy-day efforts, execution of good interval sessions, and peaking were the areas my first coach, Sam Walker, emphasized. CU's Coach Wetmore, however, considered the long run to be one of the most important elements of training, and I quickly learned how effective long runs can be in building overall aerobic fitness. By the end of my sophomore year, I had built up to a 14-mile long run within weeks in which my total volume reached 70 to 75 miles. Many of these long runs were done on Magnolia Road, a long, rolling dirt road above Boulder situated between 8,000 and 8,500 feet above sea level. Those long runs were demanding but not exhausting or debilitating. I saw huge benefits from including them and realized how important they were.

Over the years of working with Coach Wetmore, I experimented with my effort levels during long runs. Mark had a gift for getting athletes to buy into a training principle. He preached the benefits of a hard long run and would compare times from previous runs, then discuss who on the team was not putting out their best effort, thus building a psychology around the team pushing the effort. We all wanted to roll up to the finish and have Mark voice his approval of our effort. A heroic long run was the best way to prove your commitment to him and the program. To do so, I found that I was pushing myself very close to the limit, but along with that came a confidence and belief in what I was doing.

During my senior year, however, I learned my limit with the long run and the effort tied to those workouts. By this time, the long run had become my entire weekly focus. I was doing other workouts during the week and was concerned with building weekly volume, but my mindset was focused on pushing the long run. I was training well in all the other areas, but I wanted to prove to myself, my teammates, and Coach Wetmore that I owned the long run. One instance stands out for me because it ultimately sealed my fate for my senior cross country season. I typically ran 2 miles longer than all but one other guy on the team. I would get dropped off on Magnolia Road a mile before the start location for the rest of the team. I would run from behind for the first 4 or 5 miles until I caught the group. On this particular day, the day after an 8K cross country race, I was instructed to run the first half controlled and then could pick up the pace from there. Heading west, Magnolia Road gradually gains in elevation over the first half of the run, which means out-and-back long runs drop in elevation after the turnaround point. I did as instructed for about 6 miles, but then I could not resist any longer. I ended up pushing my pace for the final 13 miles, running 1:57 for 19.6 miles, or 5:58 mile pace for the entire run. Even with a moderate first 6 miles, that equates to about a 2:36 marathon effort at high altitude (more than 8,000 feet above sea level) at a time when I was several years away from building up to my first marathon and only a few weeks away from the NCAA cross country national championships.

It was an audacious effort, to be sure. That effort was not only too hard given my overall fitness, it was doubly taxing because I had run the cross country race the day before, and my body was already fatigued when I started. By the time I got to the NCAA cross country championships a month later, I was cooked. In reality, I probably burned my national championship chances up on Magnolia Road that day.

So what is the takeaway? The rest of your efforts during the week need to be treated with equal importance as the long run. Many

Rest Days

Depending on your goals and level of training, rest days—when you don't run a single step—can be a very important part of your training. That might be hard to fathom if you are a dedicated runner who is eagerly and earnestly working toward a long-term goal. But, if properly timed, days off from running allow the body to absorb training by giving it a chance to rest and recover while also clearing the mind. But the term "rest" doesn't mean you should be lying on a couch and being as inactive as possible. Instead, other types of low-intensity exercise should be encouraged on rest days—such as supplemental strength and mobility work or crosstraining—as those activities provide a form of "active rest" and activate the body's systems in different ways that can rejuvenate you. The key is not to overexert on rest days in a way that would impact your running workouts in the days that follow. Active rest can be as simple as an easy bike ride around your neighborhood or walking the dog around a local park for 30 minutes. It's also a good time to catch up on sleep, especially if the break from running means you have 30 to 60 minutes of extra time that day.

runners struggle with that mind-set. Just as I was trying to prove myself to Mark, many runners crank up the intensity during long runs to prove something to a training group, a coach, or themselves. Runners are sometimes tempted to run close to marathon race pace for most of a long run to assure themselves that they are ready for the distance. Others get caught up in a group-run dynamic and run more aggressively than is prudent. Both scenarios are easy to fall prey to, especially once your fitness advances to a higher level. At that point, you may not necessarily struggle with running a long run too hard and so may not even recognize the problem when it's happening. In fact, it's likely the opposite—it feels so good to run hard on long runs that you don't want to run slower. But you absolutely have to hold back. Keep emotions in check and your pace appropriate, and don't let long runs turn into a race effort.

I recently spoke with a recreational runner who argued that he needed to run his long run at marathon race pace if he were to have any hope of running a full marathon at that same effort. This sounds good in theory but is not as good in reality. If you are training properly and including all the other weekly elements, running the long run at or near marathon race pace will prove detrimental. Running consistently throughout the week will provide more significant gains than hammering the long run and dogging the rest of your runs or having to endure lingering fatigue from that near-race-pace effort.

Along with an overemphasis on the long run, a lack of variation is a standard practice plaguing distance runners of all levels. The idea of "long, slow distance" (LSD) was popularized by the influential coach Joe Henderson in the late 1960s, and as a result, a slow long run became the predominant approach. Many runners have fallen prey to the long run becoming simply a long easy-day effort. There is a time and a place for long, slow runs within a training program: early in the Base Phase; during a down week in a heavy-volume period; during an intense training cycle in which three hard sessions are already included in the week; or during a Race Phase, when a slow longer run is a nice complement to the week. A slower long run can also be fine during the off-season, during the Buildup Phase prior to a Base Phase, or occasionally during a Transition Phase in a period when a focus on hitting a particular intensity takes precedence. But the point is not to get lulled into running your long runs too slow on a regular basis.

Moderate-effort long runs provide huge gains over the course of a training period. The key is keeping your pace moderate so that it does not turn into a long tempo run or marathon race pace effort. Most elite athletes use the long run as another high-level aerobic stimulus, and this approach is valid for runners at all levels. Running the long run at a moderate effort, about 15 to 30 seconds quicker than a standard easy day, is an effective way to gain aerobic development. The goal is to run the long run quickly enough to stress the cardiovascular system into building more aerobic enzymes but not so hard that it affects your next harder workout. Landing on that correct moderate effort is the trick. As a red flag, if you find that you are feeling fatigued for three to four days after a long run, then you ran it too hard.

Another approach to add variety to your long run is to include a workout within it. For example, a tempo run or fartlek for 25 to 50 percent of the total run can be included to mix up the effort. Try including a 5- to 10-mile tempo run at goal marathon pace in the middle of the long run or a short fartlek followed by a few easy miles at the end. This should not be done week after week, but it can be done about every four weeks if you typically only run one or two harder workouts during any given week. This is especially beneficial if your total mileage is fairly low or if you are preparing for a shorter event such as the 5K or 10K.

Long Intervals

Long intervals, which are hard, sustained efforts at 5K to 15K race pace, are the most-overlooked and underemphasized aspect of training. This likely stems from an inherent misunderstanding of what long intervals are and what system they are meant to stimulate. Most training plans include intervals between 3 and 8 minutes in duration, but what is neglected is the appropriate intensity. This means many runners end up running their long intervals too easy, making them, in effect, just another form of a tempo run. In fact, they are meant to be run at a hard effort above your lactate threshold—in other words, at a level where your body is producing some level of lactic acid during each interval.

Reps of hard running that last from 3 to 4 minutes should be close to 5K effort, while 4- to 6-minute reps of hard efforts should be at 10K effort, and 6 to 8 minutes of hard running are ideal at a 15K race-pace effort. In the Base Phase, the intensity is less and the rest longer. Early in the Transition Phase, the effort should be at your current 5K to 15K fitness level. Later in the Transition Phase and during the Race Phase, long intervals should be at goal 5K/10K/15K race pace. So, for example, if you are hoping to run a 6-minute-mile pace for a 5K, then your 3-minute intervals during the race phase should be at 6-minute-mile pace. If you are only in 20-minute 5K shape during the Transition Phase, then those same 3-minute intervals should be executed at 6:25 pace.

Long intervals are not just a training tool for elite runners; they should be a staple for every distance runner.

The goal of long intervals is to teach your system to buffer the effects of lactic acid longer and also to use that lactate as fuel. The greatest 5K runners in the world use lactic acid as a fuel source, not simply the glycogen stored in their muscles. Those runners include long, hard intervals during the Transition Phase of their training as well as some longer intervals in the Race Phase. Long intervals are not just a training tool for elite runners; they should be a staple for every distance runner with performance-oriented goals.

Many generic training programs don't prescribe this type of workout with the appropriate intensity. It should feel uncomfortable! In fact, done properly, long intervals are some of the hardest workouts you'll do as a runner. A tempo run or fartlek can be managed, and speed work is short enough to get through, but long intervals performed properly are very tough. The good news is that if performed properly, long intervals provide some of the greatest benefits for race-readiness. By teaching your body to manage lactic acid, you prepare your system to race at a harder sustained effort.

Planning long intervals—when to do them and how—can be tricky. High school and college athletes who race almost every week—and often multiple times during a week—don't need very many additional long-interval workouts. If you are following a training program that includes hard races week in and week out, you too should avoid long intervals unless performed slower than race pace (or at race pace but with generous rest between each). Running long-interval workouts at a hard intensity along with hard racing can lead to overtraining.

I include myself in the group of athletes who missed the mark when it came to implementing long intervals. Unfortunately, it took me until very late in my running career to see the full benefit of adding them to my program. Consequently, my personal bests in the 3K (7:47) and 5K (13:25) are comparatively not on the same level as my mile (3:55), 10K (27:33), and marathon (2:09:41) best. Early in my professional career, when I was focused on the 5K, I did not do long intervals consistently or race very often. While I always included longer repeats in my Base Phase and cross country preparation, once I transitioned to track training, I simply did not include the necessary mix. As a result, I ran between 13:27 and 13:31 in the 5K around 15 times in a five-year window, although runners whom I considered my athletic peers ran 10 to 25 seconds faster. Yes, 13:30 is a solid time, but I had run 3:55 in the mile and sub-3:40 for the similar distance of 1,500 meters on several occasions. So a PR of 15 seconds faster in the 5K should have been very reasonable.

Following yet another 13:28 effort, this one at a track meet in Palo Alto, California, I remember talking with Shayne about the race, trying to figure out what was missing. Every race played out the same: I would settle into a pace that was slower than I had expected, and with about 5 laps to go in the 12-lap race, I would struggle to hold my pacing. After fighting to hold that pace but often slowing down for a few laps, I'd get to a point—usually with 2 laps to go—when I would be able to take off and finish strong. Physiologically, what was happening was that my system could not handle the lactic acid building up throughout the race, which starts almost from the onset of hard running. When this happens, you feel increasingly worse as you continue running. Your muscles begin to feel very heavy, fatigued, and sluggish, especially in your legs. That can lead to psychological fatigue as well because you feel that you are working hard to maintain but losing the battle. Once I got to the point at the end where I could go fully anaerobic and flood my muscles with lactic acid, I was fine because I did shorter, speedier anaerobic workouts all the time. But had I been doing longer intervals, I could have improved my racing fortunes by amping up during those middle laps.

Later in my career, I added longer intervals and saw very positive results in the 10K. It made me wonder what would happen if I did the same with my 5K training. Now, by 2005, I was fully dedicated to the marathon, knowing it was my best event as it related to international competition. I was coming off my 12th place effort at the 2004 Olympic marathon and the following April placed fourth in the Boston Marathon, at that time the highest finish by an American in 17 years. Although my future was set in the marathon, I still wanted to prove to myself that I could run a faster 5K than I had to date. I took several weeks off after Boston in 2005 and had seven weeks to get back into 5K track shape. I incorporated long intervals at 5K and 10K race pace every week, repeats anywhere from 1,000 meters to 1 mile. After seven solid weeks, I traveled to London to run a high-level race in the historic Crystal Palace. I ran a 13:25 5K, and although I was nowhere near contesting for the win and my time was no record, I felt a sense of satisfaction. While I believe I could have run closer to 13:10 in my career, the results in London after seven weeks of 5K-specific training and at an age where track workouts were harder to come by helped prove my theory that I had been underdeveloped in that regard in my younger years. Better later than never, both in terms of learning and improving.

Long-Interval Workouts

Here are four examples of typical long-interval workouts.

4–6 × 1,000 m at 5K pace/effort
  (2:00–3:00 rest, depending on the phase)

4–6 × 1 mile at 10K pace/effort
  (2:00–3:00 rest, depending on the phase)

3 × 2 km/1 km at 10K pace/effort for the 2 km and 5K pace/
effort for the 1 km
  (2:30 rest after each)

3 × 3 km or 2 × 3 km/1 × 2 km at 15K pace/effort for the 3 km
and 10K pace/effort for the 2 km
  (3:00 rest between each)

Long intervals should be mixed into every training phase. In the Base Phase, the interval intensity should be less and rest between intervals should be longer. As you move into the Transition Phase, long intervals must be included every 10 days during a half-marathon or marathon training program or every seven days for training plans geared toward shorter races. The key is hitting the correct effort with the right amount of muscular output: too easy, and they become a tempo effort; too hard, and you run the risk of getting overly fatigued. Landing on the correct effort takes a high level of self-interrogation. You have to ask yourself during the workout if you are truly running 5K or 10K effort. A willingness to push out of your comfort zone is critical in order to maximize the efforts and truly mimic race effort. This is where a race during the Transition Phase is helpful because not only do you work the desired physiological system but you also get a great gauge of your current fitness. You can build your long-interval workouts around the time you hit for a particular 5K or 10K race and also get a much better idea of goal race pace. In general I suggest taking more rest during longer intervals such as 1,000-meter repeats, a session of 6 × 1-mile or a 3 × 2-mile workout. The goal is to hit the desired times, not to force curtailed rest between intervals. Arturo Barrios, the former world-record holder in the 10,000-meter run, typically took 3 minutes between 1,000-meter repeats. He is a great example of someone who understood how to do solid long-interval workouts while not forcing the rest.

As I learned in my own 5K experiment, you must be willing to try new things in order to see different results. If you are consistently underperforming, then something is missing from your training. It may well be the long interval.

Speed Work

Speed work is another key component to a training cycle, and the proper timing and execution of these workouts within the scope of a periodization plan is critical. By its simplest definition, speed work is a type of training that helps you run faster. But there is more to it than that. Various types of speed work are the tools that not only help you run at a higher rate of speed but also allow your body to run efficiently under the duress and fatigue of racing situations. A runner can progress considerably based solely on the aerobic-development running that makes up the Base Phase, but at some point the runner's fitness will hit a plateau and stagnate if that's the only stimulus the body and its various systems are receiving. Appropriate speed work implemented at the appropriate time is an integral part of any well-rounded training program.

Speed work is another aspect of training where the emphasis is often out of balance when compared with the other systems—and often comes at the expense of sufficient aerobic or lactate threshold training. For example, some runners place too much importance on anaerobic speed work sessions, either because they are fun to do, because they have a knack for them, or because it seems like something they should do. Short, fast speed sessions can be thrilling but should not be done several times a week, nor at the expense of other types of workouts. Younger athletes tend to overemphasize speed work—largely because that's what's built into their high school training—while older athletes neglect it. Interestingly, considering the benefits of speed work and the physiology of younger versus older runners, it should be the opposite. The nervous systems of younger athletes—from young teens to mid-20s—are already naturally more enhanced, as are muscle strength and responsiveness and neurological timing. What younger athletes tend to lack is overall aerobic strength, which comes from a gradual increase in mileage over several years, threshold work, and sustained efforts above lactate threshold. In other words, when we're younger, it's easier for us to run fast. Therefore, emphasizing speed work at that age is not as useful as developing other aspects where the need is greater.

Older runners (early 30s to mid-50s) have the benefit of overall aerobic strength. However, as we age, our nervous systems do not fire as acutely as they did when we were younger, and muscle elasticity and responsiveness diminish increasingly. Therefore, speed work is highly beneficial for this age group.

It is human nature to tend toward the type of workout that is the easiest. When we are younger, running fast feels good. It comes more naturally, the workouts are short, and the discomfort is short-lived. As we get older, speed can start to feel uncomfortable and risky, whereas a high-level aerobic run feels controlled and sustainable, thanks to that good aerobic fitness developed through years of training.

When it comes to speed work, getting a few steps out of your comfort zone is required. The key is applying speed in the correct amount depending on the distance for which you are preparing and what phase you are in. Don't be fooled into thinking that speed-free training will lead to a race-day pace that is dramatically different than your average daily or tempo-run pacing. The consistent inclusion of quicker training stimuli (workouts faster than race pace) will help you run your fastest on race day. Remember, fast running leads to fast racing, no matter your age, ability, or background.

Fast running leads to fast racing, no matter your age, ability, or background.

So what is speed work? Speed work is fast workouts designed to help you gain more power, efficiency, and specific muscle adaptation. When new runners think of speed work, they often picture sprinting. But sprinting is a small component of speed work and is really necessary only for someone preparing for events from the 800-meter to the 1,500-meter (or 1,600-meter) runs on the track, where a top-end gear that produces all-out speed is necessary to compete. National- and world-class distance runners do include sprinting in their programs even when training for events from the 3K to the 10K, but they are the exception. For our purposes here, speed work typically encompasses workouts that are shorter than 3 minutes and are run close to 1-mile race pace effort. (For example, that might mean running 10 × 400 meters in 70 to 72 seconds if you're a 4:40–4:48 miler or 80 to 82 seconds if you're capable of running a 5:20–5:28 all-out mile.) Like long intervals, speed sessions should be included in all phases of training, with rest between intervals varying throughout the year. (In that same 10 × 400 workout, you might take 3 minutes between reps in your early training phases but 60 seconds later in your program.)

Many training plans lack the consistent inclusion of shorter-interval sessions throughout the training phases. Neglecting speed work is a mistake if you want to reach performance-oriented goals. We all have a complement of fast- and slow-twitch muscle fibers; some have more of one than the other, but we all have both. Speed work is a powerful training tool you can use to develop your fast-twitch fibers

Running Workouts

Here's a breakdown of the workouts that should be in your training regimen with brief definitions and highlights of each one.

Long Runs

Long runs are long, although the distance might vary from 8 to 22 miles, depending on where you are in your training program, your level of fitness, and your ultimate goal race. A weekly long run is a key building block of your training plan and integral to developing basic aerobic fitness. While some long runs are meant to be slow—especially early in a training cycle—some should be run at a moderate pace or have a progression-oriented pickup built into the mix. An example of a long run with a progression tweak might be turning a standard 18-mile run into 10 miles at an easy pace and the final 8 at marathon or half-marathon race pace.

Tempo Runs

Tempo runs are sustained "comfortably hard" efforts of 20 to 60 minutes run at your lactate threshold pace (roughly your half-marathon race pace). The purpose of a tempo run is to advance your aerobic fitness by stimulating the production of aerobic enzymes and also to simulate race pace. Although standard tempo runs range from 4 to 8 miles, a tempo workout with variation might include something like 3 × 2 miles at tempo pace with 90 seconds to 3 minutes between reps and can be as long as 10 to 12 miles in some instances for higher-level athletes.

continued >

Long Intervals

Long intervals are hard, sustained efforts at 5K to 15K race pace run at your anaerobic threshold. During these intervals, your body cannot efficiently process oxygen and is dealing with fatigue caused by the accumulation of lactic acid in the blood. These extended hard runs increase your anaerobic threshold, or your ability to run fast and as efficiently as possible while fatigued. An example of a long-intervals session is 5 × 1 mile at 10K race pace with 3 minutes rest between reps.

Speed Workouts

Speed workouts develop both your quickness and your top-end speed, which will not only help you race faster but also help you run better in all phases of your training. An example of a speed workout is 10 × 400 meters at 1-mile race pace with 2 minutes rest between reps.

Hill Workouts

Although easier on the body, hill workouts are a form of speed workouts that develop speed, muscular strength, good running form, and neuromuscular timing. The keys to effective hill workouts are a consistent effort and good running form. An example of a hill workout is running 45 seconds up a hill with a moderate pitch and jogging back down to the start as the rest intervals.

Recovery Runs

Recovery runs are short, slow- to moderate-paced workouts done on easy days as a way to create a buffer between your long-run day and harder workout sessions. Recovery runs are a form of "active rest" and help the body rejuvenate while flushing out any residual lactic acid from the previous day's run and still providing some slight aerobic benefit. Recovery runs might be 20 to 75 minutes in length, depending on the timing of the run within your training plan and your weekly regimen, but they aren't meant to be run as slowly as possible. Rather, the pace of recovery-day runs should be as quick as possible while still providing a recovery effect from your previous session so you can be fresh for your next hard session.

Rest Days

Rest days are the days when you give your body a break from running. One off day per week is my recommendation. That doesn't mean you should necessarily be inactive. You can still do some crosstraining or an alternative form of training that will benefit you without stressing your muscular system in the same ways that running does. Of course, rest days are a good time to catch up on sleep too.

and your ability to run anaerobically as well as neuromuscular strength and timing, which in turn allow you to run faster and more efficiently when you're fatigued.

Let me explain what the pay-off of good speed work might look like in a marathon. On race day, every muscle fiber, both fast and slow, is called into action. As the marathon continues into the later miles, slow-twitch muscles fatigue, and the fast-twitch fibers are needed to maintain the same pacing. Regardless of your aerobic conditioning, neuromuscular strength and timing are still very much required. I ran my fastest marathon in 2002 coming off a track season in which I had won the national outdoor championships in the 5,000-meter run. Why was I able to excel in a 3.1-mile race in early summer and then also in a

26.2-mile race that fall? The speed work and faster training I had done on the track in the spring helped me to fully develop my fast-twitch muscular system and quick-response neurological timing, which I then carried into my marathon training. Since I went into marathon training with my speed already highly developed, I was able to take my training to a higher level by being able to maintain a quicker pace in my workouts.

So we've established that speed work is essential to your training program. That said, no matter what your age, ability, or background, take care with how you implement it. The body adapts relatively slowly to pace, and injury is the biggest risk when including shorter-interval sessions. The urge to go out and knock out 400s on the track can be hard to resist; after all, speed work can be fun and exhilarating. However, even if you come out of a workout seemingly unscathed, you might wind up paying a price a few days later. Tendinitis and muscle strains are the most common problems that can arise. To ward off injury, start every speed session with an easy warm-up run that includes dynamic drills (bounding, high knees, lunges, butt kicks, etc.) followed by several 70- to 100-meter strides. (For a description of dynamic drills, see Chapter 8 as well as the video link at www.velo-press/champion.) From there, ease into the first reps of your workout, focusing on form and rhythm. Use only the muscular effort needed to reach your goal time for each rep, and avoid all-out sprinting to hit a desired split or final time.

Including some easy shorter-interval sessions during your Buildup Phase and more-moderate efforts during your Base Phase allows for ample time to slowly adapt. It only takes three to four speed sessions to get your connective tissue and neurological firing patterns stimulated, but you need to err on the side of caution and avoid jumping in too quickly and injuring yourself in the process. Listen to your body and bite off only what you can chew.

Hill Workouts

Hill workouts, another form of speed work, are often misunderstood or dreaded. True, hills may slow your pace, increase your heart rate, and cause some discomfort, but these workouts offer robust benefits to your running and are an extremely effective training element. Hill workouts should be treated similarly to other speed workouts but implemented less often during a training schedule.

The repetitive nature of hill workouts forces the muscular system to develop in response to the stress being placed on it, and the nervous system increases firing patterns to fast-twitch muscle fibers. Hills also increase speed endurance because of the resistance inherent to running uphill and the associated increase in heart rate. I cannot stress enough how beneficial these workouts are to overall strength and speed mechanics.

The most common approach to hill work is hill repeats. Repeats should be less than 2 minutes in duration and more consistently should be in the 45- to 60-second range. During the Base Phase, a hill workout once every two to three weeks is a good rule of thumb; during the Transition Phase once every three to four weeks. Hills can be phased out during the Racing Phase when more specific race-pace work is required.

Hills are a great way to introduce faster work into your program. Hill workouts aren't any easier to execute than other forms of speed work, but they can be easier on your body relative to other workouts. Given the fact that you are running up a hill, you are moving at a slower pace, and your body is enduring less impact. Injury-prone runners who struggle with adding faster work will find that hills provide the same stimulus with less risk.

The only hill workouts that should be done with caution are short and fast hill sprints of 8 to 10 seconds. These should be reserved for younger athletes or for someone who has already been doing hill repeats. If you have shown proficiency with hill workouts and do not have any injury issues, then you may consider short hill sprints. These can be done at the end of an easy run a couple of days a week. They should be run on a steep hill, and full recovery time should be allotted to maximize the effort of each sprint.

Tempo/Aerobic Threshold Runs

Tempo runs, or efforts that are right at aerobic threshold, are an effective way to gain overall aerobic conditioning and are a highly effective weapon in your training arsenal. A properly executed tempo run will typically mean running for 20 to 60 minutes at 80 to 85 percent of maximum heart rate—which is generally at a runner's current half-marathon race-pace effort range. That pace should be right at your aerobic threshold (or lactate threshold) based on your current fitness level, which is a given variable no matter what event you're training for. As you increase your fitness level, you'll know you are improving your aerobic threshold because it will be slightly easier to run faster at the same effort level. (Tempo-run workouts will vary in length and complexity as your fitness progresses and as you start to fine-tune your training to a particular event from 5K to the marathon.)

One reason to run tempo runs is that they help you to understand both what half-marathon race pace feels like and how it feels in relation to other race paces. For example, if you are training for a half-marathon, tempo pace will start to become ingrained in the proprioceptive relationship that exists between your mind and body. Simply put, you'll develop a knack for running that comfortably hard pace. If you're training for a marathon, a half-marathon pace will feel a tad fast, but in a good way—because you know that marathon race pace will be slightly slower. As you get more fit and get into a groove running that pace, you'll gain confidence because it will feel more natural.

From a physiological level, an even more important reason to run tempo runs is because running at your aerobic threshold (or lactate threshold) encourages the body to stimulate the production of aerobic enzymes within your blood, and that leads to a greater concentration of mitochondria, which help turn oxygen into energy, within the cells of muscles. In simple terms, it means that tempo runs help increase a runner's oxygen-carrying capacity, ultimately helping him or her become more efficient running at faster paces.

But, like long runs, tempo runs are often overemphasized or ineffectively executed. A common misconception is that there is always room for another tempo run. The Olympic approach says otherwise.

To be most effective, tempo runs require the proper complement of all the various training stimuli in a particular training phase. Like the other aspects we have discussed, an aerobic threshold (or lactate threshold) run is simply one ingredient in the recipe.

Also, tempo-run paces must be varied. While running at or close to your threshold is no doubt the best way to stimulate the aerobic system and improve your oxygen-processing efficiency, there must be a balance of work above and below threshold in order to effectively manage race-day pacing. Running at race pace is certainly important from a central-nervous-system perspective as well as to gain confidence in your ability to maintain a particular pace and develop a good sense of perceived effort, but running too many workouts in that zone can be limiting for a number of reasons:

- Ultimately, you won't be as fit as you could be if you are also implementing longer intervals into your routine. Longer intervals are run at a higher intensity than are tempo runs—which means they're decidedly harder—and force your body to respond by producing even more red blood cells.
- Your tempo pace will be limited without the inclusion of speed work. Without increasing your speed, you will remain slower overall and unable to become more efficient at faster paces.

However, when tempo runs are properly implemented within a comprehensive periodized training plan, you'll start to reap several benefits:

- Your race pace will feel much more comfortable with the addition of other interval workouts.
- You will be able to run tempo pace longer and slightly faster and feel more comfortable at race pace for any distance.
- You will have a greater margin for error when it comes to race pace if your body is accustomed to running a pace quicker than race pace and an effort harder than tempo effort.

Too often athletes run tempo runs because they are straightforward to execute. You don't have to run intervals; you don't need a track or a hill. You just go out and run at an up-tempo pace and feel like you are getting a solid workout. This is fine if you are training for a local fun run without a time goal in mind and simply don't want to suffer as much come race day. If you have a targeted goal, however, then tempo-run-focused training will not get the job done. You will get very good at running one pace with no margin for error. Many runners with whom I have spoken have had dismal marathon experiences because they have done only the traditional marathon buildup, with the standard mileage increase, long-run duration, and a few weekly tempo efforts or fartleks. The lack of comprehensive fitness is exposed on race day when they find themselves going out a bit quicker than they practiced. A complete athlete can manage a mistake such as going out 10 seconds per mile too quickly by slowing down, recovering, and still executing a solid race. The tempo or lactate threshold approach does not allow for any mistakes.

Finally, you must ensure that the effort is truly at your lactate threshold. Many runners do not know what their lactate threshold really is or have not been running long enough to have a clear perception of what that effort should feel like. They often end up running these workouts too hard. Running a tempo run too hard defeats the purpose of utilizing the aerobic system to its fullest while still efficiently processing oxygen (the lactate threshold). Running at a pace between a runner's lactate threshold and anaerobic threshold for an extended period of time simulates a near-maximal race effort and leads to greater fatigue and more muscular breakdown than is warranted.

It should be noted that running a tempo run too easy can be equally ineffective because it doesn't allow the desired physiological gains and leaves you on a training plateau that, if continued, could eventually lead to a decrease in fitness.

Recovery Days

Recovery days, which are short, easy-paced runs scheduled between hard workout days, may be less intense than other days, but don't let that lull you into nonchalance about this key session. Easy recovery runs play a significant role in training. Indeed, they should be more abundant than any other type of day in your training schedule.

A common notion associated with a recovery-day effort is that you can run as slow as you want; it's just an easy day, so it doesn't matter how slow you run. Incorrect. While an exact pace is not set in stone, as a rule of thumb, a recovery run should be as quick as it can be and still allow you to recover in time for your next hard session. In other words, not too easy. (If you're not entirely recovered from your previous day's workout, your heart rate will be higher than normal at the same easy effort level or easy pace.) The only athletes who should be truly jogging on their recovery days are either full-time professional runners with maximum mileage of 130 to 150 miles a week or someone who is new to running. An example of a group that runs recovery days very easy and sees good results is the Japanese marathoners. The Japanese have adopted the marathon as their primary event of choice and tailored a training system around a single-minded execution of marathon training. But it is important to note that they run 140 to 170 miles per week, typically by running three times a day. The 9-minute miles they average during recovery jogs makes perfect sense; without it, they would be overtrained in a short window of time.

During my marathon training, I usually ran twice a day and hit 120 miles per week consistently, with a few weeks in the 130-mile range. On recovery days, I averaged a 6:20 pace per mile. The first mile was always slower, and I would gradually work up to a 6:30 pace and finish up close to 6:10 pace. This was a solid clip, given the high altitude, but I worked at ensuring that it was never so hard that I would sabotage my recovery for the next hard workout. Knowing that I had a tendency to run a bit too hard, I would monitor my heart rate on occasion and try to keep it under 140 bpm for the majority of the run to make sure my perceived effort lined up with my actual effort.

Another mistaken notion is that it is okay to run harder on a recovery day in order to squeeze in another up-tempo run and bump your fitness just a little bit more. A recovery day is a time for your body to rebuild and refresh for the next hard session. To repeat: Run as quickly as you can while still recovering. This will take some trial and error to find the right balance for you. If you know your max heart rate—determining it through a VO_2 max test or even a basic fitness assessment test is much better than estimating it with a standardized formula—then you can pretty easily figure out whether you are running too easy or too quickly. (Wearing a heart rate monitor isn't necessary for determining your max heart rate, but it can be a training aid on occasion once you know your max heart rate and corresponding training zones.)

Early in 2004, my wife, Shayne, realized that she was running her easy days too easy. She figured it out by doing a VO_2 max text, which gave her an accurate breakdown of max heart rate and thus the heart rate she should achieve for various training zones. Previously, she would run how she felt, which typically meant very slow on recovery days. She was clear and focused on her intensity days, but recovery days for her were just about putting in the time, not a means of gaining fitness. After the test, among other tweaks, she adjusted her easy-day pace during her Base Phase. She went from running a 7:30 pace per mile to a 6:30 pace for her easy days. She also started monitoring her heart rate and pace and focused on running as quickly as she could but still slowly enough to recover from day to day. These simple changes allowed her to take full advantage of her Base Phase and elevated her fitness significantly over the course of three to four months. As a direct result of the changes, she made a big step up in performance in 2004, winning a U.S. indoor title and a world championships bronze medal in the 3,000-meter run as well as winning the 5,000 at the U.S. Olympic Trials and running a 30-second PR in the 5K.

Train Smart: A Systematic Approach

The objective of training is to consistently work your body's various systems. Thinking of training in slightly different terms may help put this in perspective. In terms of weight lifting, the various physiological systems are like the different muscle groups of the body. You can group the muscles into collections: legs, chest, arms, and core. These are like mileage, tempo efforts, long intervals, and short intervals. Imagine that you go to the gym to work on your chest for a given workout but instead decide to do arms. If you had arms on the schedule for the next weight workout, you would throw off the whole system. You would be overworking one set of muscles and neglecting another.

This simple example illustrates the difference between training hard and training smart. Yes, training should be hard and challenging; however, each workout must have its place and be executed at the appropriate effort. You might as well not do a tempo run if you are going to run it consistently too hard. Remember the mantras: Train with intention.

Every day has a purpose. Don't fall into the trap of running too many tempo runs or running them too hard. Or cheating your recovery day. Or approaching your long run like just another easy day. Training must be both intentional and comprehensive; you can't do biceps curls every other day and expect to be fully developed.

Executing your workouts correctly—training smart—means understanding the method to your madness and being thorough in your approach. That starts even before you do your first workout, with a precise goal, a plan to train you for that goal, and an understanding of and adherence to the training principles outlined in this chapter and Chapter 5. You need to be intuitive at times, tempering your intensity and judiciously applying the correct amount of effort each and every time you run. A comprehensive approach will help you reach optimal fitness and give you the opportunity to reach your ultimate running goals.

– 7 –

DIET, FUEL & HYDRATION

My recently retired father was introduced to the world of running during a simpler time. A runner in the early 1950s in Fort Worth, Texas, didn't have much technology to rely on, and gear and nutrition were not the multibillion-dollar industries they are today. Not by a long shot. As a product of the modern running-shoe revolution of the past 40 years or so, I was particularly fascinated as a young runner to learn that he did not have running-specific shoes. Instead, he ran in generic athletic shoes that fit snugly and held the foot in place but offered little or no cushioning. There were none of the specialty cushioning elements that we take for granted now—no air bags, gel inserts, Hydroflow, Rebound, adiprene, or even basic ethylene vinyl acetate (EVA). Shoes offered just a thin rubber outsole between your foot and the road, which meant a force 10 times your body weight pounded that rubber down in every stride. He says he would often get bone bruises from stepping on stones while running because there was so little between his foot and the ground, plus the road quality of the 1950s was not the same standard we have now.

The new dynamic has brought the importance of diet, hydration, and fuel to center stage.

My dad's high school team would often run several miles from his high school to the nearby golf club, where they would promptly ditch their shoes in the bushes and run barefoot on the soft grass. Running barefoot on grass was a treat when compared with the discomfort that accompanied athletic shoes at the time. Runners trained hard back then, no doubt about it. This was before Jim Ryun burst on the scene as a world-class miler in the early 1960s but was still a time when daily 10-mile runs or 20 × 400-meter repeats were commonplace for a high school runner.

My dad's nutrition and hydration choices were based less on gaining a competitive edge in running than on surviving a tough day of work, school, and training. His family owned a laundry-service company, which was close to 10 miles from their home. My grandfather would drop him off not far from the house so he could run exactly 10 miles to the laundry. He would then work a full day at the laundry, eating potato-chip-and-mayonnaise sandwiches on white bread and putting down several Cokes to quench his thirst. He and his brothers discovered that salt tablets helped them better endure the long hours of extreme temperatures that came with being surrounded by hot dryers and no air conditioning; there were no other sports nutrition products available at the time.

He ran well enough to get an athletic scholarship and compete in college for his first two years before promptly losing his scholarship for getting married. He failed to read the fine print in the scholarship, and they yanked it the following semester. Running was a means to an end for him—a way to help pay for his education and a competitive outlet but hardly the lifestyle choice it is for many of us today. There were no recreational road races or specialty running stores as we know them today, nor were there social running groups as there are now. Given the lack of comforts and social incentive, it is no wonder that he stopped running for 25 years. There was just no reason to run if not for competitive purposes. Fortunately, his interest was reinvigorated when I found the sport as a 12-year-old. He returned to running and went on to complete several races, including his first full marathon at age 53.

My father's experience in the sport reminds me of where we came from, simple days when the emphasis was on training hard because training was all there was. Unquestionably, the progress we have seen technologically, scientifically, and nutritionally has enhanced the sport and activity of running. But training is still by far the most important element to ensure the desired results. When I look at training and the other ancillary components and how they compare in terms of importance and relation to success, here is how I break it down: Training is 85 percent; diet, hydration, and fuel make up 10 percent; and injury prevention is the final 5 percent. Although these elements are important, you can't hydrate, stretch, or massage your way to a personal best. There is no way around the hard work of training. The 10 percent we will look at in this chapter—namely diet, hydration, and fueling—stand behind your training, supporting and enhancing it. Poor choices in these areas can negate the 85 percent of training.

Modern Sports Nutrition: A Caveat

Diet, hydration, and fuel for runners have become serious topics of interest only recently. Unlike training, which has its basis in a half century of validated practices, how and when to fuel and hydrate—and with what—represent an emerging science. The new interest in these topics has much to do with the shift in the participant base in endurance events overall, which now encompasses people of all ages and abilities, many of whom are new to running. This influx of recreational participants into the sport has prompted the growth of new industries to serve them. As these runners have developed a heightened awareness of diet, hydration, and fuel, a new category of products has emerged to meet and (literally) feed that interest.

New runners bring new questions, and the new dynamic has brought the importance of diet, hydration, and fuel to center stage. Twenty-five years ago, it was all about the training; 15 years ago, it was footwear technology and synthetic fibers; and in the past few years, hydration and fuel have joined footwear at the forefront of the industry. Just as we've seen a lot of new types of shoes emerge, we've also seen a huge increase in products within the recovery, fuel, and hydration category. When I was in college in the early 1990s, we had the original PowerBar products and the standard Gatorade in a small range of flavors. Today there are hundreds of varieties of bars; flavors of drinks; and various gels, chomps, chews, beans, and other forms of electrolyte replacement products readily available on running-store and grocery-store shelves.

It's been a mostly positive evolution for the sport and the entire endurance category. The flourishing of these products has made recovery, fueling, and hydrating more accessible, more prominent, and more likely to be included in daily training and race planning. Prior to the development of all these products, it was harder to develop the right nutrition and hydration strategy for training and racing; in fact, most runners didn't even consider such a strategy.

That said, educate yourself so that you can employ these products wisely. As much as packaging and advertisements sometimes say otherwise, there are no gimmicks in running—no magic shoes, no special fibers, and no secret supplements that will improve performance. What these secondary aspects will do is enhance your experience and allow for a greater potential for success. In other words, they will aid your performance rather than define it.

It's human nature to want a quick fix or an easy answer. When I was in college, I got caught up in a few of the dietary fads of the time that promised better performance. When the fat-free craze was popular, I was not immune. I found myself eating massive amounts of carbohydrate and protein and neglecting fat intake. A full portion of pasta followed by a dozen biscuits was a common meal during my junior year of college. I was certainly getting in enough carbs, but without the fat, I never felt satisfied and, worse, was neglecting a critical fuel element necessary to distance runners. Desperate to improve, I was looking to dietary components to help. Not only did my diet limit my performance on a daily basis—especially in longer races—but it also greatly inhibited my ability to recover on a day-to-day basis. As competitors, we seek out ways to be better, and diet surely seems to promise improvement. But while diet and other secondary aspects are important and necessary ingredients in the training recipe, they are the pinch of salt or touch of sugar, not the flour and eggs that is hard training.

With that perspective in mind, let's take a closer look at how diet, fueling, and hydration can play a role in moving us closer to our goals. My purpose is not to cover all the complexities of these topics. Diet, hydration, and fuel are massive, unwieldy, and controversial topics that have been handled more comprehensively in books entirely dedicated to the subjects. Rather, my hope here is simply to highlight those areas in each category that can have the biggest impact on your training, racing, and recovery.

Time Is of the Essence

During my dad's marathon training, he would occasionally remark with wonder about a day when he just felt "in the zone," as he put it. By that he meant days when he felt really good and could push as hard as he liked with ease and lack of consideration for the fatigue in his legs. These times were never predicted and often came on easy days. He was always caught by surprise by the fact that he felt so good. I would encourage him to recall what circumstances had preceded the run: What time of day did he run, what did he drink, what did he eat, when did he eat? A pattern emerged. Without question there was a reason he felt so good, and it had much to do with his fuel and hydration choices. While he might not have realized it, on the days when he was listening to what his body was craving and fueling it at the right times, his training went notably well.

Some athletes have very good instincts about what their body is craving and when to fuel. For the rest of us, however, it's not so intuitive. Many athletes struggle with not just how to eat but how to time their eating to maximize their training.

There are a lot of popular strategies when it comes to when to eat, ranging from the "three square meals a day" and "clean your plate" ideas to backloading calories to eschewing hearty meals altogether, instead "grazing" on mini-meals and healthy snacks throughout the day. The last idea is based on the premise that your body can't (and shouldn't) go for long periods without refueling. Grazing is about having consistent caloric intake so your body doesn't run out of glycogen and go into a quasi-starvation mode in which it will obtain fuel from other sources and start breaking down muscle. This notion goes hand-in-hand with the concept of training flow and the idea that your nutritional needs and fueling plan should be integrated into your daily process and not an environment where you need to binge on larger meals or large quantities of fluid at any given time. Grazing allows your body to avoid a peak-and-valley cycle and the mental and emotional side effects that often go with hunger pangs or dehydration—such as irritability, fatigue, or a lack of mental acuity—and can disrupt workouts.

Grazing can help you run better on a daily basis because there's less chance you will be glycogen-depleted or dehydrated when you run. If you are an early riser who runs as soon as you wake up, or if you run before lunch or in the early evening before dinner, there's a good chance you've burned through your glycogen stores and are dehydrated if you haven't been constantly fueling and rehydrating. Avoid that by making sure to take in 150 to 200 calories and a glass of water the moment you wake up, an hour before your lunchtime run, and during the afternoon hours before you end your workday. These intermittent snacks along with smaller meals support more effective training.

The idea of continual fueling and rehydrating coincides with your race-day fueling and rehydrating strategy as well. If your body is used to taking in small amounts on a regular basis, it will be accustomed to processing it during a race. But if you typically run without grazing or rehydrating in advance, your body will have a harder time adjusting midrace if you drink 5 to 8 ounces (about 150 calories) of a sports drink or consume a gel or other fueling product. Too, if you stick to a more traditional eating and drinking plan in your daily life, going long periods between larger meals, you'll limit the effectiveness of your recovery and train your body to create fat stores with the excess calories consumed in those meals.

Proper and predictable fueling helps you to manage how you will feel from day to day.

As discussed in Chapter 3, creating a predictable environment around your training is important. What, how, and when you eat and drink is an important part of that process. Proper and predictable fueling helps you to manage (and take some control over) how you will feel from day to day. Why does this matter? In order to execute a proper training buildup to a particular event, it is imperative that your training builds upon itself week after week. Workouts, long runs, and increasing volume work together to ensure the necessary fitness gains, and they build off each other. When you follow a proper training program, you can't afford to be "off" physically, at least not for long. Yes, there will be days that just don't come together for various reasons related to work, family, travel, and illness or simply the effects of hard training. But this makes it even more critical to ensure that you are able to execute your day's training and hit your mark on all the other days. Smart, predictable fueling strategies help make that happen.

Diet: Managing Calories During Training

Does your race goal include losing weight or managing your weight during training? This is not uncommon for many runners, sometimes for health reasons or to reach what they see as an ideal racing weight. There is a common misconception that by skipping a meal here or there, you can reduce your daily caloric count or that you can backload your calories. Backloading calories is a tactic sometimes mistakenly employed by young runners, and even some seasoned runners consider it a quick means to drop a few pounds and reach their racing weight. The idea is to limit what you eat during the day, keeping the calorie total low, and then eat a large dinner. Along with my fat-free experiment, during college I slid into a pattern of not eating enough during the day and then consuming the majority of my calories at dinner. This was not by choice but rather due to the circumstances of college living and poor daily planning. In college, I tended to eat more calories at the end of the day due to the schedule of courses and having team practice at 3 p.m.

This pattern was reinforced by the accessibility of inexpensive volume-based restaurants around Boulder. My college teammates and I enjoyed gorging ourselves at a local restaurant named Café Gondolier that had an all-you-can-eat pasta-dinner special twice a week. Not only was it inexpensive, but it was really good homemade food, with thick pasta noodles and tasty sauces. Inevitably, the amount of pasta we could consume became another form of competition. You would order one plate of pasta at a time, and the goal was to ingest as many plates as possible. Three was a normal night, four was a good showing, five was limited only to a few brave individuals, and six was downright dangerous. You never ordered a drink or appetizer because that threw off the whole pay-breakdown of $6 apiece and also because it would take up unnecessary space in your stomach. Our tactic was to order two plates as quickly as possible so we could avoid slowing our rate of consumption and confuse our sensory systems so they wouldn't figure out we were full before we had shoved at least three plates down our throats. When I look back, I have to laugh at how ridiculous the whole scene was.

For some, it was about competition; for me, it was a function of back-loading calories. I was ravenous from not eating enough throughout the day and from hard training. Studies have shown that backloading calories leads to higher body fat. A study I read used two control groups that ate the same amount of calories in a 24-hour period, the difference being that one group spread its calories throughout the day via five smaller meals, and the other backloaded 70 percent of its calories during the last part of the day. All the subjects were weighed at the start and end of the study, and their body mass index was also taken to measure body fat percentages before and after the study. Weight remained relatively unchanged in both groups because most were eating their normal daily caloric needs. But the group that backloaded calories had an increase in overall body fat, while the other group lost body fat percentage.[1]

You may not be frequenting all-you-can-eat buffet restaurants or struggling with gorging yourself to get your money's worth. But some of you may limit calories at points during a day in hopes of cutting down on overall calories or simply are not following the good habit of eating every couple of hours. Regardless of body fat, the problem with going long periods without eating is that it limits recovery, slows your metabolism, and leads to dehydration. When you don't eat for an extended period, your body shifts to starvation mode, slowing your metabolism to hold on to calories and fat. When you get to this point, you begin to

1. M. Lombardo, A. Bellia, E. Padua, G. Annino, V. Guglielmi, M. D'adamo, F. Iellamo, and P. Sbraccia, "Morning Meal More Efficient for Fat Loss in a 3-Month Lifestyle Intervention," *Journal of the American College of Nutrition* 33, 3 (2014): 198–205, doi: 10.1080/07315724.2013.863169.

burn muscle instead of fat and thus limit the recovery process within the muscle itself. Also, when you don't eat frequently, you lose the ability to retain water. Solid food helps the body absorb fluids. Along with tasting good, food is our fuel, and a consistent intake is required to ensure proper recovery. This is even more important when training. Skipping meals or going long periods without eating will not work if you are trying to train hard at the same time. No matter what time of day you train, you must adapt your system to eat throughout the day.

Fueling and Hydration

Continual rehydration and fueling are crucial in marathoning (and a sound idea for runners pursuing any kind of race goal). As someone coming from a track and cross country background, I was generally aware of the need to drink fluids during longer races, but I wasn't familiar with the best strategies for fueling during longer races. For my first 15 years as a runner, I never once took in any type of fuel—or even water—during a race because it was not an option. There are no aid stations in cross country races or on the track, and they are not necessary in races that last less than 45 minutes. It should come as no surprise, then, that I had to learn how to refuel (ingest calories) and rehydrate (drink water and replenish electrolytes) during the run when I started running the marathon.

My first marathon experience was at the 2002 Chicago Marathon, and, as is the case for many first-time marathoners, it provided a wide-ranging learning experience. Although I had not yet raced even a half-marathon, I had been diligent in my preparation and felt ready to race 26.2 miles.

I had worked hard at devising a race-day fueling plan. I was proficient with my fueling needs on a day-to-day basis and in training, but racing a marathon was a new experience. As I said, up to that point, I had never consumed fluids during a race; I had not felt that I needed to because the longest race I had run was a 15K. Consuming calories during short races is unnecessary, and hydration is only moderately necessary, depending on the conditions. For a marathon, however, a solid race-day fueling and hydration plan is critical, and I took this aspect seriously. My plan was take in as many calories as possible via my drink solution. Due to my slight build and lean muscle makeup, I did not store muscle glycogen very effectively and therefore needed to ingest more calories during a race than other athletes in order to maintain my energy level and perform to my aerobic potential.

I decided to focus more on fuel and less on electrolytes or volume of fluids. Although energy gels were starting to become a big deal, I had not experimented with them much at that point, and my plan was to take in only liquid fuel during the race. I knew my body well enough to know that at a 5-minute-mile pace, I was not going to be able to easily digest anything other than fluids.

In researching various ready-mix and powdered formulas, I chose one with what I thought offered the best combination of a higher-calorie concentrate and sufficient electrolytes. I practiced with it on my long runs during the late summer and early fall in Boulder. August and September can be quite warm on Colorado's Front Range, and most of my long runs were done in 70-degree weather. I didn't know it at the time, but that proved to be an inherent flaw in my planning and conceptualizing compared with the reality of Chicago's weather on race day.

By the time the October race date came around, my body was prepared for a warm-weather marathon. My system had become accustomed to taking in fluids during runs in warmer conditions. When the temperature is moderate, say in the mid-50s to upper 60s, your body doesn't need excessive blood flow to warm up the working muscles or lower the overall body temperature. When the temperature falls outside those ranges, it becomes more dependent on the individual's physiology of blood flow throughout as it relates to digestion changes.

For the better part of three months, I had done my due diligence and prepared properly by teaching my body to absorb fuel during workouts with intensity. I had practiced taking in fluids—the exact formula I was planning to use in Chicago—during my weekly long runs and during my longer tempo runs, which were close to goal race effort about once every 10 days. However, I failed to consider the fact that the race might be 20 degrees cooler than all of my training runs. The temperature on the morning of the race in Chicago was 36 degrees. It was expected to rise into the low 50s, but a steady 10- to 15-mph breeze coming from the north was going to make it feel colder and provide more resistance in the course's final miles.

Cool to cold weather is great for slowing the loss of electrolytes on race day but not so beneficial for absorption of fuel. It takes blood to digest, so the harder you are working aerobically, the more blood flow is diverted away from the gut and to your muscles and skin. The reason not to refuel in a race with a peanut-butter-and-jelly sandwich is because it cannot be digested efficiently. The digestion process takes blood flow and fluid and both are compromised when you exert yourself at race pace.

Race morning, when the starting gun went off, I stuck to my pacing strategy and fueling plan. As an invited athlete, I had the added benefit of having my own bottles out on the course at 5K intervals. We prepare the mixture the night before the event, and the bottles are placed on the course on race morning. Each runner is assigned a specific place on the aid-station tables, so you know exactly where to look for your bottles every 5K. The solution in my bottles was exactly the same as it had been during my previous 15 weeks of training.

At the first two aid stations, I drank my premixed fluids and felt good. But by the 15K mark, I noticed I was not thirsty, was drinking less than planned, and was burping up my lemon-lime solution for 3 miles after drinking it. The marathon is not an event in which you can play catch-up if you don't properly fuel and hydrate early in the race. You can't skimp on the early aid stations and make up for it when you feel thirsty later in the race. Your thirst sensation is a good indicator, but it often gets compromised when you are working hard aerobically or are distracted by all that is going on around you during a race. The key is to consistently refuel and rehydrate during the entire race, regardless of thirst, not to overdrink but simply to be consistent.

I kept charging along and dealing with the burping and lack of thirst, but through the first half of the race I wasn't drinking the full amount of fluid in my bottles. Instead of taking in 8 ounces, I was struggling to get in 5 or 6 ounces. A difference of 2 ounces doesn't sound like much, and it isn't if you are just walking around the mall or going about your daily life. But if you're running a marathon at your maximal race pace—no matter whether you're trying to break 2:10, as I was that day, or shooting for 2:50 or 3:20—missing 2 ounces of fuel during the middle 15 miles of the race is devastating, a little like skipping the all-you-can-eat buffet after not eating for three days.

My goal was to take in 550 calories for the entire marathon. Missing out on 2 ounces of fluid for five aid stations added up to missing out on 140 calories total, or 25 percent of my planned intake. Those missing 2 ounces caused a significant deficiency in fuel, which I desperately needed at the pace I was trying to run. Although the cool temperatures lessened the need for higher levels of electrolytes, that weather also caused me to burn more fuel than normal at race pace as my body worked to stay warm. Miles 23, 24, and 25 were the slowest of the race, and I knew that I was right on the edge of completely blowing up. In the end, I held strong and finished the race in 2:09:41, tying Alberto Salazar for the best debut marathon in American history. (Ryan Hall lowered that American debut record with his 2:08:24 in 2006.) It stands as one of my proudest achievements.

Although it had been a very successful debut, I knew that I had underperformed because of my fueling. I was glad I had chosen a higher-concentrated-carbohydrate solution because I had got in more calories with less volume, but had I adjusted the solution slightly, I could have taken in more at each station, thus increasing the total amount of fuel and calories for the marathon as a whole. Looking back and comparing that race with my other marathons, I realized that what made that race harder than it should have been was that I had not tweaked my race-day plan to compensate for the unexpected weather. In sum, I was too rigid in my training preparation to respond to different conditions.

Although those final 4 miles to the finish line were tough, the hardest part was yet to come. Those who have run a marathon know what I am about to share. Once I stopped and sat down, it was all over for me. I tried to get my warm-up pants on but was struggling to even bend my legs. My quads and hamstrings were destroyed. I had averaged 120 miles a week for two months heading into the event, topping out at 135 miles for a few of those weeks. My body was as physically ready as it could have been. I had the muscle strength to cover 26 miles at my desired pace, but I didn't have the fuel to manage that pace for 26 miles. When I crossed the finish line, I was utterly out of gas, and my muscles were not going to work until I drank and ate. It took me 45 minutes to walk two blocks from the finish area in Grant Park back to my hotel. My legs literally would not move properly. I wound up running six more marathons in my career, and never again did I experience that level of post-race lockdown.

I am fully convinced that this aftereffect was due not to pushing myself harder or digging deeper but rather to an ineffective race-day fueling plan. Whether it is your muscles locking down due to lack of glycogen or cramping due to lack of electrolytes, it comes down to how well you manage your intake during the event. I did many things right in my race-day fueling and hydration approach to my first marathon attempt. I practiced in training leading up to the event by taking in the fluid I was going to imbibe on race day, and I had a solid plan. But I fell short in making adjustments to the plan based on the race-day conditions.

Taking in less of the higher-concentrated mixture might have been okay had I supplemented it with something else. I should have shifted to the water and Gatorade on the course to give my system a break from the higher-concentrated drink. That way I would still have gotten fluids, carbohydrate, and electrolytes into my system, but not as much at one time. Your body will tell you what it needs if you pay attention. I was paying attention and could tell I was off but did not adjust as needed. I am not recommending rash decisions early on or overreacting. But I do recommend a backup plan that includes subtle deviations from your plan when necessary. Even subtle changes can make a big difference. The key is having a plan to begin with, then being open to adjust slightly as you go.

The Science of Hydration

In the spring of 2004, I visited the Gatorade Sports Science Institute (GSSI) just outside Chicago. The experience dramatically changed my perception of the importance of hydration. Up to that point, I had a general understanding of hydration and the overall importance of it but not to the extent that was required, as had been evidenced by my experience in the Chicago Marathon.

The GSSI is a fully functional lab with metabolic testing, VO_2max testing, gait analysis, and sweat-rate/sweat-content analysis. Along with product development, research, and testing, the lab also works with athletes of varying ability levels to quantify the effectiveness of its products. Like many athletes, I experimented with a variety of products during my training (although there were far fewer then), but I inevitably turned to Gatorade out of convenience and availability. It wasn't until my visit to the GSSI, however, that I fully understood the science behind the product. The type of sugar, concentration of carbohydrate, and electrolyte blend were all scientifically tested. I learned about the rates of gastric emptying and precisely what carbohydrate concentration percentage I should be ingesting during races.

My Chicago Marathon had been run in atypical fall conditions, with a blustery wind and cold temperatures. As described, I had tried to drink but struggled with my stomach feeling full even with a 5K gap between fuel stations. This was partially due to the cooler conditions and my body redirecting blood flow to my working muscles to keep warm, but I learned at the GSSI that it was probably also due to the concentration of carbohydrate in the product I had been using that day. My plan to drink all my calories had made sense in theory, but in practice the high-carb solution I had chosen was simply sitting in my stomach and not being absorbed.

Taking in calories and refueling on the run is great as long as the fuel is being absorbed. Otherwise you are simply filling up your stomach and slowing your refueling process unnecessarily. Everyone has a threshold based on their individual makeup and the effort at which they are running. It's a lot easier to refuel when you're running slowly, but the closer you are to running at threshold pace, the slower the stomach empties. The GSSI used stomach catheters to test gastric-emptying rates. (Simply put, they stuck tubes down athletes' throats to measure how quickly the product left the stomach and then compared that to water.) Although I was not tested to determine my own gastric-emptying tendencies, I gained practical insights that helped guide my caloric intake during marathons. For example, I learned that a 6 percent carbohydrate solution is the highest concentration of sugar that can be added and still exit the stomach as quickly as water. Over 6 percent, the rate of gastric emptying will be slower than that of water. Some athletes can afford to push that percentage higher because they are not running at a level of intensity that slows gastric emptying significantly. In triathlon, for example, you can take in solid fuel on the bike due to the lower heart rate and subthreshold intensity. The higher the heart rate and closer to threshold you are, the less blood gets allocated to the stomach for digestion.

There are many good fueling products out there, and, as with training tendencies, we all have a unique makeup and ability to ingest, digest, and absorb various fuel options. In my latter marathons, I opted for a mix that allowed me to take in more of the electrolytes I needed along with that all-important 6 percent carbohydrate solution.

Hydration and Perspiration

Sweating and endurance events go hand in hand. But we all have a slightly different physiological makeup and therefore have different rehydrating needs during a race. Not only will race-day weather conditions play a role in your performance, but how you react to those conditions—depending on whether it's cool or warm, dry or humid, for example—will dictate how much you sweat and how much you deplete your electrolyte levels.

During my visit to GSSI, they tested my sweat rate in a testing chamber set at 80 degrees and 40 percent humidity. Testing showed that I was losing more sodium than expected in my sweat and therefore needed to replace that during my runs and races. My sweat rate was acceptable, but the content of the sweat, specifically the ratio of sodium to water, was very telling. Losing more sodium than normal can simply be a function of the season. When temperatures are cooler, we lose heat mainly from the tops of our heads. Sweat loss is less significant, however, because we tend to lose more electrolytes that way. It might seem counterintuitive, but it is a function of efficiency. As temperatures warm and our bodies adapt, we become more efficient at losing heat throughout the body and not just the head, but we also lose fewer electrolytes as the body learns to regulate the sweat loss. In cooler temperatures, electrolyte concentration in sweat tends to be greater because cooling the body is less of a priority, so sweat has a lower percentage of water. My losing excessive sodium in the GSSI test was in part due to the fact that I had not run in 80 degrees in almost six months. But when scientists at the institute studied the content of my sweat, they deducted that I still lost higher-than-normal sodium content despite my lack of heat adaptation. This was an important finding that I was able to factor into my summer training in the lead-up to the Olympic marathon in the sweltering conditions in Athens. As related in the next section, to compensate, I altered my rehydration strategy for that event by adding supplemental electrolytes to compensate for the added loss during the hot conditions.

Lessons from a Warmer-Than-Expected Marathon

Hindsight is 20/20, as I learned from my experience in Chicago. At the 2004 Olympic Marathon in Athens, however, I was able to adjust my race-day fueling plan based on the weather conditions and this time get it right. Athens was warm and humid during those Olympics—so warm that organizers planned the men's and women's marathons for early-evening starts. The idea was that temperatures would fall as the event went on—a much better situation than starting in the morning and having temperatures rise as the races went on.

Several months prior to the race, the USATF and the U.S. Olympic Committee (USOC) had coordinated a marathon symposium for each of the six qualified athletes and their coaches. We worked with renowned physiologist Dr. Dave Martin and other top USOC sports scientists who had been to Athens several times to study ground temperatures, humidity, wind patterns, pollution, the layout of the course, and elevation gain. The symposium was very informative and prepared runners to give extra consideration to the unique challenges the Athens marathon would present. As in my first two marathons, the 2002 Chicago Marathon and the 2004 U.S. Olympic Trials Marathon, I took

Daily Hydration Plan

Many runners are walking around poorly hydrated. There is an urge to make up for this lack of consistent hydration by drinking a large amount just before exercising. While this is better than not hydrating at all, it does not get the job done. Before you pound a lot of fluids and then head out the door assuming you are hydrated, remember that it takes about 20 minutes to absorb ingested fluids. Early risers in particular need to consider this added time for absorption before they simply jump out of bed and hit the roads.

Here is a better way to handle hydration.

- *Pre-run:* 20 to 24 ounces of water or electrolyte-rich sports drink, but avoid ingesting a large amount of carbs before a run. That simply adds more sugar and unnecessary calories. Your light pre-run meal has more than adequate calories for daily training.
- *During exercise:* 4 to 6 ounces of water or electrolyte-enhanced sports drink (depending on weather conditions) every 20 minutes for runs longer than 75 minutes. For runs in the 50- to 75-minute range, 8 to 10 ounces over the entire run will suffice. For runs under 50 minutes, hydrating during the run is not necessary unless you are an excessive sweater or conditions are very warm. But there is no harm in bringing a small bottle with you on shorter runs.
- *Post-run:* 24 to 32 ounces of an electrolyte-rich sports drink. This is the best time to drink a carbohydrate formula. Read the label and be mindful of the electrolyte content; many "recovery" products have fewer electrolytes than you might think and are very high in calories and protein.

continued >

> Protein is important to rebuild muscles, but electrolyte replacement should be the first and foremost aspect of rehydrating after a run.

a diligent approach to race-day hydration and fuel planning for the Olympics. I practiced several times each week taking in fluids during longer runs and longer marathon-effort workouts and developed a solid plan for my fluid intake. I adjusted my race-day planning based on the information I had received from the USOC symposium and through the testing at the GSSI after the Olympic Trials. Unlike my first two marathons, which had both been in cooler conditions, I knew I had to factor in the heat and subsequent electrolyte loss at the Olympics, not just the need to refuel.

I had used a different formula in the Olympic Trials race than the one I had used in Chicago and had a much better response in terms of fluid absorption. The solution contained lower levels of carbohydrate (sugar), which allowed it to empty from my stomach more quickly and thus get absorbed into my system. Granted, I was running at a more controlled pace at the Olympic Trials, so that might have been a contributing factor as compared with the effort level I was exerting in Chicago. However, I still managed to win the trials race and run 2:11:42, so the race was not run slowly. Plus, I felt much stronger throughout the race and immediately afterward. I decided to use the same formula in Athens.

With temperatures in Athens expected to be in the 90s at the start of the race and knowing that I lose a higher concentration of sodium in hot weather, I adjusted the amount of sodium and other electrolytes I planned to ingest. I knew that while a fast time was less likely in Athens, the heat would demand a harder effort and lead to a higher level of electrolyte loss through sweat. My plan was to take in 10 ounces of the formula at every 5K aid station. That added up to about 75 ounces during the race, given that I would most likely not be inclined to take in 10 ounces at the 40-km mark, a little more than a mile from the finish.

For three weeks prior to the Olympics, the U.S. marathon team sequestered itself on the island of Crete to try to adjust to the weather conditions. During that period, I realized I would need to increase the amount of electrolytes I took in during the race. Ten ounces every 5K was already a pretty aggressive target, and I knew expanding it could increase the likelihood of gastric discomfort. So instead of just drinking more, I decided to add more electrolytes to the mixture in my bottles. I did not add more carbohydrate or increase the concentration but rather just added more electrolytes through electrolyte packets, upping the sodium, potassium, and magnesium levels by an additional 20 percent. I felt confident about the plan and knew that if I executed that piece, I could run close to my potential.

Having a good fueling and hydration plan is critical to success in longer events because it eliminates rash decisions when you are not thinking properly amid the anxiety leading up to a race or during the race itself. It also allows you to keep your mind occupied for portions of the marathon with the simple task of taking in fuel and fluids. It breaks the event up into smaller segments, helping you wrap your mind around the race and not feel so overwhelmed. Taking control of areas within your means is key. Focusing on smaller, manageable pieces within the race frees your body to simply run.

During the Olympic race, I followed my plan with precision and could feel my body responding. After navigating through the first two water stations, I started paying closer attention to others around me and how much they were taking in. I recall seeing Kenyan Paul Tergat, who at the time held the marathon world record of 2:04:55, grab his bottle, take a few sips, and throw it down. I also recall Gert Thys, a South African runner with a 2:06:33 PR, taking in only water. When I saw that, I knew I would surely see them again 10 miles down the road. I will share more about that marathon experience in Chapter 9, "Racing," but in terms of fuel and hydration, I could not have managed better than I did that day. I doubt any of the 104 athletes who started the race drank more than I did that day, and it showed in my results. I finished 12th in the race, and although my finishing time of 2:15:26 was relatively slow, thanks to the sweltering hot conditions, I fared better than many runners who had entered the race with much faster PRs than mine. Tergat, the pre-race favorite, finished a disappointing 10th in 2:14:45, while Thys wound up 16th in 2:16:08.

Optimizing Hydration

Hydration is commonly overlooked or misunderstood by many runners, enthusiasts and elite athletes alike. Sometimes athletes get distracted by new fads, "miracle" products, or gadgets and fail to create a properly balanced state of consistent hydration. A lack of consistent, daily, targeted hydration creates a host of unwelcome issues: limited recovery, unpredictable workout results, and increased potential for injury.

Our muscles crave water, as does our vascular system. Sometimes runners experience a struggle to breathe that is different from the feeling that comes from not being fit or going out too hard in a race. Rather, it feels like air getting caught in the upper part of the chest and often occurs in warm conditions. This is a result of dehydration. Another unwelcome side effect of dehydration is a higher-than-expected heart rate. If your heart rate is 10 to 15 beats higher than usual under the same effort level and conditions, then you could be dehydrated. Blood flow is affected by improper fluid intake. Blood becomes increasingly viscous as dehydration sets in, resulting in that shortness of breath. As the body of a muscle loses fluid, it gets tighter and can start to fail. That's why hamstring and calf cramping issues are common when you become severely dehydrated. With better hydration comes better blood flow throughout the body and thus better flow of oxygen.

As I've emphasized throughout this book, finding rhythm and predictability in your daily routine is key to training. Hydration must be folded into the same line of thinking as the timing of your training, a sustainable day-to-day running schedule, and consistency in meal planning. This is especially true the harder you train, the longer the race you are preparing for, and the higher the volume of overall work.

Optimal hydration is critical to achieving optimal performance. I have trained with and coached too many athletes who are missing the mark with their hydration. Our bodies are very good at adapting to the conditions we place them in. That means you can get away with a lot and still run. But "getting away with" something is not the same as setting yourself up for success. Don't slip into the cumulative dehydrated state that many athletes suffer from. Be proactive in your hydration planning and routine: Think ahead, bring fluids with you, and make these things part of your overall plan for your day.

The benefit to effectively hydrating in training is that your body is ready to absorb fluids efficiently on race day. And that is critical. Once the starting gun goes off, your body must be efficient because blood flow will be increasingly diverted away from the gut and to the leg muscles. Blood is diverted not only to provide oxygen and fuel to your largest muscles but also to keep your body cool in warmer weather. Warm conditions present a double whammy because now not only is more blood allocated to the muscles as the effort goes up on race day, but even more is diverted away from the gut to regulate your temperature. This is why efficient and effective absorption of fluid is crucial on race day. Practice hydration faithfully during training.

Prepare Like a Champion

If you are going to put enormous effort into something and sacrifice your time, energy, and resources, then you might as well prepare like a champion in all areas—including your training and race-day hydration and fueling plan. It begins in training, creating for your body an optimal environment to absorb your training through proper diet and hydration, but it also has to be at the top of your mind in the days leading up to the race and during the race itself.

I have seen runners train well and make the necessary sacrifices only to get to race day and choose that moment to take a lackadaisical approach to hydration and fueling. While not advisable, it's easier to make mistakes and recover from them in a shorter race such as a half-marathon, but your hydration and fueling strategy cannot be an afterthought for the marathon. For shorter events, the bigger concern is having sufficient hydration for proper muscle functionality and oxygen-carrying capacity. Refueling is less of a concern in shorter races because glycogen depletion generally isn't a factor in distances up to a half-marathon. Once the time and distance go up, however, the emphasis on fuel requirement and subsequent planning goes up substantially.

There are three keys to race day fuel/hydration management.

Practice taking in fuel and fluids during training: Practicing your race-day nutrition and hydration plan helps your body get used to drinking and ingesting calories on the run. (Some runners react harshly to products available on the course, so know in advance what you'll have access to aside from water.) This practice makes you go through the physical and mental routine that you'll need for race day—for example: when and how you'll pick up a cup at an aid station and how you'll drink it.

Have a race-day strategy for fuel and fluid intake: Understanding what your body needs during a specific race is important. Decide how many calories and how many ounces of fluid you'll need to ingest per hour of racing. Consider the course and how your intake plan might vary at different points. Is the first part of the course shaded and the second part more sunny? Are there more hills at the end than the

Marathon Race-Day Nutrition Plan

Dialing in your fueling and hydrating is important for any strong race and crucial in the marathon. Use a modified version of the suggestions below for shorter distances from 5K to half-marathon.

Pre-race Fuel

3–4 hours before start

- 300–500 calories of easily digestible foods (e.g., a bagel with butter; toast with jelly; oatmeal; two small pancakes with a little syrup; fruit such as cantaloupe, pineapple, or strawberries)
- Avoid high-fat foods such as bacon, sausage, or nuts; whole grains; and high-fiber foods.
- If you are a coffee drinker, stick to your routine and typical intake.

1 hour–75 minutes before start

- 100–200 calories (e.g., an energy bar that you have used in training, a banana)
- Avoid high-calorie bars or meal replacement bars.

Pre-race Hydration

- 20–28 ounces per hour. Consistent hydration and nursing fluids leading up to the start is critical.
- Sip water or a low-calorie electrolyte blend. (Food ingested during pre-race fueling should meet your calorie needs.)
- Electrolyte tablets are a great way to top off electrolytes.
- In the hour leading up to the event, switch from water to something with electrolytes.

continued >

Race Hydration and Fuel

- 8–10 ounces every 3 miles (2–3 cups at every aid station). The majority of your intake should be a sports drink because of its electrolytes and calories; use water as a supplement.
- If stomach issues arise, switch to water only. Skipping a few stations of sports drink and just taking water helps calm the stomach.
- Even in the early miles, hydration is critical.
- Even in cool weather, hydration is critical.
- Consider taking a gel, chomps, or sports beans (caffeinated if you wish) between miles 8 and 9, 16 and 17, and 21 and 22.
- Take the gel or other nutrition with 4–6 ounces of water. Do not take it with a sports drink, as that could add too many calories at once.

beginning? Also consider the conditions where you have been training and how your race location might be different. Will it be warmer or cooler? Dry or humid? Will you sweat more or less than you did during training?

Be nimble, adjusting your race-day nutrition and hydration plan as needed: You might have a good idea of what the conditions are supposed to be like, but if the weather changes or something else comes up (e.g., a last-minute course change, a headwind you didn't anticipate, a start from a different wave than anticipated), you'll have to adjust. Understanding what changes you need to make takes a blending of art and science as well as trial and error, but making them correctly can improve your results.

Get It Done

Hydration and fueling may represent a small percentage of the bigger training picture, but they can have a major impact, especially if improperly executed. Don't let 10 percent of what's necessary to run a marathon ruin the other 90 percent. Diet, daily nutrition and hydration, and race-day fueling and hydration must all be considered and planned for.

I've endeavored to give you a start here, but it is only that. I urge you to do more research and, most importantly, experiment early in your training. Consider connecting with a dietitian and taking a critical look at your daily intake and breakdown of calories. You may find that, like me, you are taking in enough calories, but a larger-than-appropriate allocation of those are dedicated to Pringles. Some folks don't realize they are eating more than they should and, until analyzed, do not even know to cut back.

Most runners are not as diligent as they need to be with their day-in, day-out hydration. Others don't practice taking in fuel and fluids during training and therefore run into various gastric issues on race day, when nerves, early rising, elevated heart rate, sweating, and working hard all come in to play. It takes practice to ready your system. It takes a concerted effort to plan meals and think about what you are taking in. If you have a busy day ahead and know you will struggle to find time to eat, then bring food with you—pack a snack or an energy bar. Going six hours without eating makes you feel lousy and forces your body into a starvation state where it then holds on to every calorie possible. If you have a long run followed by a day of activities, then plan for that; allow yourself time to eat properly, or you will compromise your recovery from the long run.

It seems so simple, but more people struggle with this piece than they do with training and racing. Here's the bottom line: Give your body every opportunity to feel good. Eating the correct foods in the correct amounts (small meals and snacks) at the correct times (throughout the day but especially before you run) and hydrating properly on a regular basis take time to figure out. But doing so is well worth the effort and will pay off on race day.

– 8 –

INJURY PREVENTION, MAINTENANCE & RECOVERY

In Chapter 1, I shared a story about how I missed several months of training during my freshman year in college because of an extended struggle with IT band syndrome. What should have been a short lapse in training or not even an injury to begin with wound up becoming not only a physical challenge but a drawn-out situation that created emotional and psychological setbacks as well. I went from feeling capable and confident in my abilities while posting one of the best workouts in the school history to questioning running in college altogether, all due to that injury.

I know now that most if not all of the consequences could have been averted had I employed a smarter approach in my daily protocol and responded more quickly once the issue manifested. But at the time, I had no proactive plan for injury prevention, did little preventive stretching, had less-than-optimal hydration, employed no warm-up and cooldown routines, and had no understanding of what it meant to listen to my body. I also did not comprehend how to treat the source of the problem.

Many minor maladies, annoyances, and injuries are entirely preventable if you build proactive injury-prevention measures into your training.

The bottom line is that my naïveté was responsible for my downfall. Happily, I got wise after that injury and developed a far more holistic program, which helped keep me healthy throughout my career. Like many runners who run full time, I still suffered some physical setbacks in my professional career—including Achilles tendinitis, a partial calf-muscle tear, plantar fasciitis, quad tendinitis, a torn joint capsule in my toe, and chondromalacia patella (the painful inflammation of the cartilage under the kneecap)—but I never again missed a season or an important event due to an injury. I was able to minimize each of these injuries with a concerted and ongoing approach to preventive measures, early detection, quick response, and the proper alterations to my training.

Unfortunately, distance running historically has a high frequency of injuries. Recent studies suggest that more than 60 percent of runners are injured every year. That's an astonishingly high number, but it's not entirely surprising. During the recreational running boom that has seen participation continue to soar since the 1970s, running has been boiled down to a rather simple activity. There's a notion that all you need is a pair of shoes, shorts, and a T-shirt and you can go running. That's true, as far as it goes, but it also vastly oversimplifies all the ancillary components that keep you out there.

Injuries might be an unfortunate aspect of running, but they're not inevitable. In fact, many minor maladies, annoyances, and injuries are entirely preventable if you build proactive injury-prevention measures into your training.

Many recreational runners give little thought to injury prevention. But if you are training toward a goal, following a training program, or working with a coach or training group, then injury prevention should be an essential part of your program and included in your daily and weekly routines. A cyclical approach in this area will not work; even small lapses in the inclusion of preventive actions can lead to injuries. You must take measures every day to ensure that you stay healthy.

This is not a function of living in fear of injury. On the contrary, being proactive in your injury prevention frees you mentally and emotionally to train even harder. Confidence is derived from the fitness and strength you've built along with the preventive measures you've engaged in. With an ongoing approach, not only will you fend off many common issues, but you will also be more in tune with your body, more apt to pick up on subtle changes and adjust accordingly. You will be equipped to bounce back more quickly as well. When a routine is established and your body is in check, it responds more efficiently and effectively.

Yes, you will have some pain and discomfort from time to time—that's an inevitable part of running—but actual injuries should be rare if you are following the right kind of program. Most injuries start as small irritations that develop and evolve into something full-blown. The key is to identify and address an issue before it becomes an injury.

In this chapter, I will discuss how to prevent injuries or keep a small issue from developing into something more severe. I will describe measures I found most beneficial, cover best practices for specific problems, and explain when to turn to an expert for help.

What You Can Do Yourself: Proactive Prevention

Injury prevention starts with a thorough, honest self-assessment—your physical makeup, where your strengths lie, where you have physical weaknesses. Do you have some obvious vulnerability? Have you suffered recurring issues in the same area? We are not all created equal when it comes to structural and muscular makeup; running gait; foot stability and mechanics; core strength; and pelvic, lumbar, and structural balance. Certainly mechanics can be altered and strengthened to allow for more efficiency, but there is only so much we can change. This is not discouragement but rather a wake-up call to insist that you step back, take stock, and ensure that you are proactively doing all you can to promote healthy muscle, develop strong yet not overly taxed attachments, and maintain correct structural alignments while also having an effective response to small common issues so they don't transition into full-blown injuries.

Establishing a Daily Routine

Just as with other aspects of training discussed in this book, taking a proactive, intentional approach to injury prevention is vital. Stretching, good hydration, a proper warm-up and cooldown, and self-massage should be made part of a habitual routine. Daily self-maintenance not only sets you up to prevent or manage discomfort but also helps keep you acutely aware of the state of your body. Furthermore, my experience has been that mind and body are more responsive to rehabilitative actions if these things have been practiced as part of a preventative routine. In the case of hydration and practicing taking in fluids during your long runs, such practice makes your body more efficient at actually absorbing those fluids during a marathon. If you practice a fueling plan in training, then come race day, when you really want your body to respond quickly and effectively, it will not let you down. I have found that the same holds true in regard to the body's responsiveness to rehabilitative actions.

The good news is that engaging in a daily routine does not have to be a massive time commitment and, in fact, can be quite simple.

Stretching

What is the biggest secret to injury prevention? Stretching. Every day.

I have told you that there are no gimmicks, no secret workouts; well, this might just be the one secret in the book. Stretching is not hard and does not take much time, but it is the single most effective means to promoting muscle health and staying injury-free.

Opinions on stretching vary; mine comes from personal experience as well as what I witnessed in other athletes whom I trained with at the highest level. I would be remiss if I did not mention that stretching is something of a controversial topic, and some runners are adamantly opposed to it. Experts don't agree on it, which adds to the controversy; different studies show different outcomes. But in many cases, ineffective or improper technique is to blame for an injury that arose due to stretching. Yes, stretching can be done too aggressively or executed at the wrong time. Aggressive pre-run static stretching is the most common mistake. If you stretch when your muscles are cold, you are pulling on the attachments rather than loosening the muscle. Aggressive post-run stretching with a focus on flexibility can likewise tend toward pulling on the attachments. If you have had a bad experience with stretching, I encourage you to try the routine I suggest below.

What is stretching really about? Let me first clarify what it is not about: It is not about range of motion; it is not about becoming more flexible; it is not a function of strength or balance. Stretching as it relates to running, performance, and injury prevention is about muscular health, and the two key functions to think about in regard to stretching are recovery and muscle regeneration. Stretching in terms of injury prevention is about enhancing blood flow into the muscle body and loosening the fibers that are either damaged from the training or bound together from the excessive stress they are being put under. When you stretch, you promote both of these aspects as well as gaining a few other secondary benefits. Stretching is by and large the most effective means of promoting muscle health—after all, a recovered muscle is a healthier muscle.

Thinking of stretching in terms of flexibility is dangerous. This approach can actually create an injury or promote the loss of functional tightness. The type of injury-prevention stretching that I suggest finds the balance between stressing the muscles slightly and creating enough tension to allow for the regenerative elements to take effect and creating excessive tension that leads to tendon strain or overly flexible muscle groups.

A healthy muscle includes functional tightness; it has some "pop," or spring. An ultraloose or flexible muscle is not an effective muscle for longer-distance running. Nor is an overly tight one, from which many runners suffer. Training leads to muscle damage, damage leads to tightness, and tightness leads to injuries. Most runners do not suffer from muscle strains except in the calf or upper hamstring. Although those type of injuries do occur, the most common running injuries are repetitive-use maladies such as tendinitis, plantar fasciitis, IT band syndrome, chondromalacia patella, shin splints, and lumbar-rotational issues that lead to piriformis syndrome or glute problems. By and large, the most injuries are caused by the repetitive motions of running with either tight muscles or poor pelvic alignment. A regular stretching routine helps prevent these issues by keeping muscles loose and lessening the strain on attachments.

Taking a proactive, intentional approach to injury prevention is vital.

Your pre-run routine should include a few light upper-body stretches aimed at generally loosening up your body for the motions of running plus some light quad and calf stretches. The hamstrings and adductors can be temperamental when not warm and easily strained if stretched too aggressively pre-run. I learned this on my own while trying to get my body ready to run during periods of high-mileage training, but I also

Pre- and Post-run Routines

While I was a collegiate athlete, I had the opportunity to take part in a three-day symposium at the U.S. Olympic Training Center in Colorado Springs with numerous other promising young distance runners. We were put through a battery of tests such as running-gait video analysis, core strength testing, and body-mass testing as well as nutritional talks and overall training discussions. Aside from recalling the discomfort of the VO_2max testing process vividly, especially because the kid who was doing the test before me collapsed on the treadmill right before I was set to get on it, the aspect that stuck with me more than anything else was what I learned about the importance of pre- and post-run routines.

After one of our easy runs, we went through a detailed program of how to stretch properly and what stretches to include. Until that point, I had stretched sporadically and without intention. I did not think of it as part of my training or the best way to keep from getting injured. At the time I went to this camp, I had only made it through one semester injury-free, so the timing was perfect, and the instruction resonated profoundly.

Below is the routine I adapted from that seminar. It is not exhaustive, but it is effective and was a big reason I was so healthy during my competitive career. I strongly suggest you develop a similar routine that can be done after every run. Proper form is key to safe and effective stretching. All of these stretches can be viewed at www.velopress.com/champion.

Standing

Hamstring: Prop one leg on a flat surface a little lower than hip. Keep knees straight and standing foot, hips, and torso

continued >

facing forward. With back straight and chin up, lean forward into the stretch, holding for 20 seconds. Rest 5 seconds, and repeat 3 times for each leg.

Quads: Bend right leg back and grab with right arm, keeping hips forward and back straight. Pull right leg toward butt to create more stretch, making sure to keep knees aligned. Hold for 20 seconds, rest 5 seconds, and repeat 3 times for each leg.

Standing IT band: Cross right leg over left leg, and bend forward at the waist. Tuck chin toward chest, and let arms hang down. Hold for 30 seconds, rest 5 seconds, and repeat 2 times on each leg.

Calf: Prop front of foot on a small step or curb and, using full body weight, stretch for 1 minute with knee straight, then 1 minute with knee bent. Switch legs and repeat.

Abductor: Spread legs approximately 4 feet apart, with toes forward, and bend forward slowly to a 90-degree bent position, with back flat and head up. Hold for 20 seconds, rest for 10 seconds, and repeat twice. Next, gradually walk hands on the ground toward right leg and hold 20 seconds, then walk hands toward left leg and hold 20 seconds.

Sitting

Glutes: Sit on floor with legs straight out in front of you. Keeping left leg straight, cross and bend right leg over left leg and hug it against chest until you feel the stretch in the glute. Hold 1 minute on each leg.

Sitting IT band: Sit on floor with bent knees and both feet flat on ground. Lift right leg up, and cross it over left leg, resting right anklebone just below left knee. Hold 45 seconds to 1 minute. Repeat with other leg.

gained valuable input from various sports-medicine experts and coaches. (See the sidebar "Pre- and Post-run Routines" for more details.)

Post-run, you can focus on slightly more rigorous stretching. This does not need to be a long routine—10 to 12 minutes is all the time you need. It is important to hit all the major muscle groups: hamstrings, quads, calves, IT bands, abductors, glutes, piriformis, and hip flexors. Also try some upper-body stretches to open the rib cage and loosen the abdomen and psoas. Develop a routine that is easy to follow, one you don't have to think about and simply include as part of your post-run ritual. Do it regularly until it becomes a habit, and you'll reap the benefits.

Maybe you don't feel that you have an extra 10 to 12 minutes. If you are that pressed for time, I recommend cutting a run 8 minutes short and stretching for 8 minutes after it rather than not stretching at all. I appreciate the desire to squeeze in as much training as possible during your window of time to run, but stretching is vitally important to muscular health.

If you truly do not have time for a post-run stretch, then the next-best option is stretching before bed each night. It's not ideal, but it's better than not stretching at all. You may need closer to 15 minutes because the muscles are not going to be as responsive as they are right after running. Typically, however, they are still warm from your day's activities, so you can get in some effective blood movement and loosening of the congealed fibers.

Hydration

Including effective hydration in your daily routine is not only critical to overall training and racing performance but also an important component of injury prevention. Effective hydration has a clear and direct impact on muscle health.

On the other end of the spectrum, ineffective hydration—or chronic dehydration—results in tight muscles, which either lead to muscle-related issues or inappropriately increase the workload of tendons and other connective tissues. Injury prevention starts and ends with stretching, but without a solid hydration regimen, stretching and the other forms of soft-tissue manipulation outlined in this chapter will not be able to do their job to promote healthy muscles. These things are definitely interrelated.

How can you ensure that you're properly hydrated? Make a habit of drinking water periodically throughout the day, paying special attention to your intake before and after training sessions. Health experts suggest that the average person drink at least eight 8-ounce glasses of water every day, but you'll need more than that if you're training. As part of your regular routine, I'd recommend drinking a glass of water the moment you wake up in the morning and making sure you drink a glass immediately before and after running. What you drink during a workout depends on what kind of running you're doing. If you're doing a long run, you should practice your in-race hydration strategy, either by carrying your fluids or by stashing them along your route. If you're doing intervals on a track, be sure to have a bottle of water so you can drink small amounts between reps.

The most obvious indication of being well hydrated is that you're urinating several times every day, and your urine is colorless or pale yellow. If you are continually thirsty, you are urinating infrequently, or your urine is dark yellow, it means you are likely dehydrated and possibly chronically dehydrated.

Warm-Up Routine

The warm-up and cooldown are afterthoughts for many athletes, or are viewed as a means of padding total mileage for the week rather than fortifying the body against injury. Slow to moderate runs don't typically necessitate a separate warm-up session, but starting out with a mile of very slow jogging followed by a series of easy dynamic movements to loosen the legs, hips, shoulders, and arms can be helpful. However, warming up with 1 to 3 miles and dynamic drills before a harder session or race is crucial to enhancing a workout's overall effectiveness. There are a myriad of physiological dynamics that prepare the body to exert itself at a higher level of intensity. This is not just a muscular process but also a cardiovascular one. A warm muscle performs better than a cold one, and warm muscles are less susceptible to injury. As the body warms up and blood flow to a working muscle increases, less strain is placed on the tendons, ligaments, and other connective tissue, thus reducing injury potential in both the muscle itself and the attachments. Increased blood flow through your system also allows for a better transfer of oxygen. Without an increase in heart rate and breathing prior to a workout session or race, you limit the effectiveness of the workout itself. Jumping into a hard effort spikes the heart rate and puts the body into aerobic shock; often the body does not reset until the heart rate drops back down significantly following a workout or after the race.

The key to an effective warm-up is developing a routine, and as we have discussed, the body loves routines. The focus is on preparing the cardiovascular system for the stress it is about to undergo as well as preparing the muscle groups to be loose and ready. You need to develop a program that works for your ability level and specific goals for a session or race while retaining the basic elements.

Here are a few simple yet essential elements involved in the warm-up that prepare the body for the workout and complement your other injury-preventing measures.

- *Jogging:* 1 to 3 miles at a very easy pace, well below normal easy-day effort.
- *Light stretching:* After the easy jog, do light stretching for 5 to 10 minutes. This is not the time to test your flexibility with all-out

static stretches; rather, hit all the muscle groups with an abbreviated version of the same routine used post-run.

- ***Dynamic drills:*** Dynamic drills are an effective way to get the body moving and increase range of motion. Individual research is important in order to find the right combination, mechanics, and execution of drills. Common drills include butt kicks, bounding, high knees, grapevines, slow skipping, straight-leg shuffling, running slowly backward, and hamstring kick-outs. See the sidebar "Implement Dynamic Drills into Your Warm-Up Routine."
- ***Strides:*** Strides are 50- to 75-meter pickup sprints at the end of your warm-up. These should not be all-out sprints. Do four to six after your warm-up run and drills, with the first few at medium effort and the next two to four at a harder effort. Think of them like going through the gears in a manual-transmission car, where you start controlled and build up over the length of the 50 to 75 meters. Full walking recovery should be taken after each stride.

The more intense the race or workout, the more critical the warm-up. Stand outside a warm-up facility at a major track meet and watch the athletes get warm and loose; the sprinters take a good hour before they are ready. Even when comparing those competing in a mile with those racing the 10K, you will see a discrepancy in the warm-up routine. The more intense the race is going to be from the onset, the more critical it becomes to have your cardiovascular and muscular systems fully warmed up. As you go up in distance, your warm-up should get shorter and less intense, but it shouldn't be any less important.

Cooldown Routine

Although easy to execute, a proper cooldown routine is often ignored by runners, either because it does not seem necessary or because of eagerness to complete a workout session. If you've done a hard workout

Implement Dynamic Drills into Your Warm-Up Routine

Taking 10 minutes for a handful of dynamic drills during your warm-up routine can help get your body moving and increase your range of motion for the workout you're about to do. Dynamic drills, done consistently, can also lead to improvement in your running form, neuromuscular timing, and stride cadence. There are many drills you can incorporate into your routine; the most important factor is doing them consistently.

Each of the drills below highlights one or more aspects of good running form and accentuates them through repetitive motion, which trains the body to become comfortable with that movement so that it can become part of your typical running mechanics. These drills can serve as a dynamic warm-up routine after a 10-minute easy jog before your regularly scheduled run or workout, or they can be completed after a run to reinstate the notion of running with good form while fatigued. Go to www.velopress.com/champion for a visual demonstration and further instruction.

Forward Arm Circles with Skip

Why: This drill loosens the upper body and opens up the lungs and diaphragm. The skipping helps increase blood flow and continues to warm up the body to prepare for the workout.

How: With an upright torso, gently start skipping forward at a slow pace and comfortable cadence. At the same time, swing the arms forward in big circles with arms straight. Do 2 to 4 reps of 50 meters.

continued >

Side-Skip Arm Circles

Why: This drill develops lateral strength and agility necessary to stabilize the body and maintain single-leg balance during forward running motion. Specifically, this drill works the glutes, hip flexors, tensors, abductors, and psoas muscles in ways that are otherwise neglected in forward running.

How: With an upright torso and level head, move laterally in one direction by alternately bounding with your legs spread and your legs together. Swing your arms overhead in an opposite pattern to maintain balance. Do 2 to 4 50-meter reps to the left and right, facing the same direction for each lateral movement.

Rolling Walk

Why: Rolling your feet at a slow, deliberate pace allows you to get full range of motion and maximum flexibility from your feet and lower legs.

How: Walk 11 to 20 strides, concentrating on rolling your foot from the heel through the midfoot and the toes, paying special attention to flexing off your extended toes as you finish each stride.

Grapevines

Why: This drill loosens hip flexors and glutes and increases hip and leg and gluteal mobility while also using lateral strength required to run with good form.

How: Standing upright with your head and torso facing forward, move laterally in one direction by placing your trailing leg in front of the lead leg. Then move the lead leg in that same lateral direction and place the trailing leg in front of the lead leg. Maintain a fluid motion with your arms rotating in the opposite direction from the legs. Do 2 to 4 50-meter reps to the left and right, facing the same direction for each lateral movement.

A-Skip

Why: This drill develops calf and foot strength needed during the toe-off phase of the gait cycle while also stimulating neuromuscular timing for running with high cadence. It also accentuates the high-knee action of the lifted leg during a running stride.

How: Skip with a moderate leap off one foot, return to the ground, and immediately leap off the other foot, maintaining a compact arm swing as if you were running. This slow-action drill should have a staccato rhythm. Do 2 to 4 50-meter reps.

Hamstring Extensions

Why: This drill increases mobility of the hamstring and gluteal muscle groups and enhances forward hip extension necessary for running fast with efficient form.

How: With an upright posture and straight legs, alternately flick one leg forward while reaching with the opposite hand to lightly tap the extended foot. Focus on form, not speed, as this will wind up being a variation of a slow-moving skipping drill. Do 2 to 4 reps of 10 extensions on each leg.

Butt Kicks

Why: Butt kicks engage the hamstrings, accentuate the recovery portion of the running gait, and improve leg-turnover cadence.

How: While running in place, try to kick yourself in the glute with your heel on each stride. Focus on keeping the rest of

continued >

your body still and simply flicking your lower leg backward. If you're not making contact, you need to improve your dynamic range of motion. Do 2 or 4 reps of 15 kicks with each leg.

Bounding

Why: Bounding increases foot, calf, and hamstring muscle power and develops single-leg stance stability necessary to maintain fluid running form while fatigued.

How: On a flat or very slightly downhill slope, alternate thrusting into the air off one leg in an exaggerated skipping motion. The focus should be on a powerful leap into the air and a quick (but not superfast) cadence. Your arm motion should be synced to the opposite leg's action, holding steady for the brief moment that you're off the ground. Do 3 to 4 reps of 10 leaps on each leg.

High Knees

Why: The high-knees drill accentuates knee lift and glute and hamstring power, which are keys to running fast and efficiently, as well as powerful and efficient leg drive.

How: Taking short steps with a very quick cadence, alternate thrusting knees upward until your thigh breaks a plane parallel to the ground. Focus on soft, flat foot strikes near the ball of your foot while using your core to lower your leg slowly instead of letting it crash to the ground. Do 2 to 4 reps of 15 lifts on each knee.

that includes aspects of fast, powerful running or long running at the same pace, it's important to follow a basic cooldown routine. If you've run long at relatively the same pace, your body gets into a mechanical rhythm by using the same muscles and movement patterns in repetitive fashion. Light jogging, easy strides, and static stretching can help loosen those muscles and engage other muscle groups to help disrupt that repetitive rhythm as the body returns to everyday movements for walking, sitting, and other nonrunning actions. (It isn't necessary to complete a thorough cooldown routine after easy runs, but I recommend adding semirigorous post-run static stretching sessions a couple of times per week.)

- *Jogging:* Just as with the warm-up routine, 1 to 3 miles of light jogging at a very easy pace can do a body good after a long run, hard workout, or race. If you have run moderately hard to hard during your workout, an easy jog will help you relax your form and posture a bit, giving those main muscle groups a break. For easy- to moderate-run days, it is not necessary to run extra mileage during a cooldown, but you can implement a cooldown of sorts in the final segment of your run at an easy pace.
- *Strides:* Doing two to four 50- to 75-meter pickup sprints after a hard workout, run, or race helps fully stretch warm muscles during the dynamic movements of running. As with pre-run warm-up strides, the goal isn't to go all out for the entire distance. Instead, build up your speed, hold it for a few seconds, and then ease back to a jogging pace. Full walking recovery should be taken after each stride, especially because your body will be taxed from your run, hard workout session, or race, and you will likely have an elevated heart rate.
- *Static stretching:* If you are going to engage in static stretching, the time to do it is after your run or workout, when your muscles are warm and more pliable. The goal is to loosen muscles and start the process of flushing out lactic acid and other post-run by-products but not to reach maximal levels of flexibility. In other

words, thorough stretching is good, but not to the point of acute pain or risking injury.

Foam Roller/Massage Stick

If you are an athlete with a bias against stretching, then it is imperative that you become comfortable with self-massage tools such as a foam roller or massage stick. There is an abundance of tools available that are wonderfully effective in promoting muscular health. If you are not going to stretch, then daily self-massage is necessary. Even if you do some stretching, there is still a benefit to including self-massage in your routine.

Foam rolling is effective in flushing out muscles, removing toxins, promoting new blood flow, and realigning muscle fibers. However, it does not address the elongation of the muscle, which is one of the primary advantages of traditional stretching. By elongating muscles, you help encourage less tension on the tendons. The tendons bear the brunt of the impact protection if the muscles are fatigued or tight. A combination of stretching and foam rolling is the most effective way to contribute to muscular health, but rolling alone is much better than nothing and can dramatically improve the blood flow and fiber alignment, which leads to effective recovery. I recommend 15 minutes of self-massage or 15 minutes of foam rolling as time permits.

As with stretching, you should develop a short yet effective self-massage routine that you can do without much thought. A foam roller is especially effective for the quads, IT bands, glutes, and upper back. The low back is riskier with the roller because you have to maneuver your body in a way that can put you in a vulnerable position. Some areas are harder to target with a foam roller due to its size; a massage stick offers a better option for the calves, hamstrings, IT bands, and quads.

Self-Assessment and Diagnosis

Pain Versus Discomfort

Say you feel an unusual sensation somewhere on your body. Is it pain or discomfort? As you train to reach your running goals, you are likely to feel a certain level of discomfort on an ongoing basis. Muscular soreness, lactic-acid buildup, dehydration, or other training-related symptoms are part of hard training. How do you know if what you are experiencing is pain that is the sign of an injury or something that could lead to an injury?

By the most simple definitions, discomfort is an uncomfortable feeling that subsides once you start running or shortly thereafter. Pain, or the precursor to an injury, is the type of ache that does not get better as you go but rather stays the same or worsens while running.

But defining pain and discomfort is not as cut-and-dried as that and, worse, can lull you into a false sense of security. Discomfort can shift and become an injury if not addressed. You can have a mild case of tendinitis that hurts only when you start running but subsides after a mile, and so you surmise that it is not a potential injury. But tendinitis can quickly become a serious injury if not dealt with swiftly and directly. Likewise, sore or tired quads that ache but don't hurt could be considered merely a discomfort but can be the precursor to IT band syndrome. Slotting pain into categories—real pain or mere discomfort—can lead to ignoring something in the early stages when prevention is key. Think of discomfort as a signal to be alert.

A stress fracture that I developed in my foot after some ambitious steeplechase training most certainly developed over time. I had felt discomfort in that area for a few weeks but generally ignored it. The actual facture happened during a track workout. About 50 meters into a 400-meter interval, I knew something was dreadfully wrong. The pain was so sharp that I shot up into the air as if I had been stabbed in the foot.

Sometimes the pain is so significant that you know for certain there is a big issue, while other times it is less obvious. The less-than-apparent issues, such as the ache I experienced building up to this fracture, are the ones that take more practice and proactive self-monitoring.

Let's be honest: Most of us try our best to run through issues and do whatever we can to just keep training. This often includes ignoring a problem altogether and hoping it goes away. Let me save you frustration down the road: This is a very bad idea. Pain, soreness, discomfort, aches, and throbbing should never be ignored. Yes, discomfort is part of pushing your body to perform at a higher level. Yes, muscle soreness within reason and managed properly is a good thing. But both pain and discomfort have consequences if not addressed and can turn into larger problems that are much harder to remedy.

Pay attention, listen, and respond. The process of injury prevention starts with you.

Response Time

When something feels off, how do you respond? Most people respond quickly if something hurts badly enough. They take a few days off, make an appointment with their therapist or specialist, or head to the local running shop for advice. This is appropriate, but more often than not, the issue has existed for a while, and the athlete failed to recognize it, ignored it, or assumed it would go away. Most things do not go away; they get worse. Where most athletes falter is when the issue is in the beginning stages. The key is recognizing the subtle changes early and responding quickly. This takes a high level of introspection. Training hurts, and our bodies experience aches and pains along the way. Be discerning when something subtle crops up. Don't assuming that a problem will go away on its own. Better to address it and find that it is nothing than to continue to train in hopes that it will turn around. Small adjustments in your treatment and training load can fend off a small issue.

Imagine your Achilles tendon feels tight after a workout. Instead of continuing to trudge onward, take the time to stretch diligently and implement post-run ice therapy for several days. If the tightness persists, consider adjusting your

Think of discomfort as a signal to be alert.

next workout. For example, if you had speed work or a hill workout on the plan, consider running an easier session and be sure to have your next long run be on a flat course. This is one of the ways you must listen to your body and think about whether it makes sense to continue training or whether you should back off slightly. Further aggravating a slight ailment can either quicken the path to an injury or, at the very least, increase the delay in becoming fully healthy. Small adjustments are part of the art of training. You should constantly be adjusting to the feedback your body is giving you and responding accordingly.

For example, say your legs feel overly fatigued for a few days. Be proactive. Perhaps a massage, some time with the foam roller, or a new pair or different model of shoes is the solution. Or maybe your feet are sore from wearing lightweight trainers for the first time. Go back to your daily trainers for your next workout, and add some extra calf stretching and rolling your foot with a golf ball. If you pay close enough attention, your body will tell you how to respond.

No response is the most dangerous. If you do not allow for adjustments and do not respond when something is hurting, then it will probably turn into an injury. An athlete whom I worked with recently went through this issue. His IT band started hurting on the side of his knee at the attachment. He was reluctant to tell me about it because he was so focused on his goal that he did not want me to adjust his training. This went on for several weeks, during which I unknowingly gave him some tough workouts, including a particular hill-repeat workout, that exacerbated the issue. He kept hoping it would just go away, but instead it developed into a much bigger issue. He ended up with a stress fracture on the head of the tibia due to all the added strain and pulling on the bone where the IT band attaches. What could have been a week or two of altered training (but still running and training) turned into three months of no running whatsoever.

Be smart, and be ready to respond and make adjustments to what your body needs. More stretching, more rest, a massage, some treatment for a specific spot, icing a slightly inflamed tendon, paying attention to the life of your shoes—these are the small but important responses that are required in order to stay injury-free. Injuries happen; how and when you respond to them is the key. I never missed an important race over the course of 10 years. Yes, I had injuries, but they were caught before they shifted to become so serious that I could not train or work through them relatively quickly. Do not let small things develop into bigger problems.

Find and Treat the Source

It is all too easy to focus your attention on the apparent injury or the symptom that is causing you pain. Treating the symptom is certainly part of the process, but without pinpointing and addressing the root of the problem, you will only prolong the issue. Most (but not all) symptoms are a function of another issue. For instance, quad tendinitis is a function of very fatigued or tight quads. It is not necessarily a function of the tendon itself but rather what is going on in the muscle that attaches to that tendon. Likewise, Achilles tendinitis is commonly a function of very fatigued or tight calves. Plantar fasciitis is also a result of tight calves, tight Achilles, and tight arches. I have discussed IT band syndrome and how it is often the result of tight quads or pelvic misalignment. High-hamstring issues are most often due to misalignment of the pelvis, causing the hamstring to be longer than it should be. Shin splints (acute tenderness along the front of the shin) result from having tight calf muscles that cause more stress on the front of the lower leg.

Chondromalacia patella is a result of the quads firing incorrectly and causing the knee to track improperly. Ankle tendinitis is caused by severe overpronating or running on very uneven ground.

So while you might be struggling with an apparent symptom, there's a good chance that it is a result of some other type of dysfunction or injury elsewhere in your body. This is not a hard-and-fast rule. Sometimes the muscles just cannot manage the stress that is being placed on them, and they get strained or slightly torn. (For runners, this is more common with the calf, but it can occur in other muscle groups.) But 90 percent of the time, there is a different and deeper root cause.

While training for the 2004 Olympic marathon in Athens, I developed a severe cause of quad tendinitis. I knew from studying the course profile that the marathon was going to be challenging. After starting with a slight decline, it rose 720 feet between mile 6 and mile 20, only to drop back down a few hundred feet over the final 6 miles to the finish at the historic Panathenaic Stadium.

In my attempt to go to the Olympics as well prepared as I could possibly be, I overdid my training and included too much hill work. Along with hill repeats, I did most of my long runs and midweek medium-distance runs on hilly routes as well. It was too much; my quads could not handle the additional impact and fatigue, and a tendon in my right leg took the brunt of it.

My approach was aggressive and a bit reckless. The inflammation and discomfort became acute enough to force me to stop training altogether for 10 days. A full 10-day break with physical therapy was not the ideal way to head into the Olympics six weeks down the road, but I had no choice.

Luckily, my ability to self-diagnose my ailments was good at that point in my career. I knew exactly what was going on, which in turn gave me confidence in my recovery. It was a lesson learned in the nick of time. If I hadn't taken that 10-day break to get healthy, the problem likely would have become exacerbated, and I either would have arrived at the starting line injured or had to sit out the Olympic marathon altogether.

If you address only the point of pain rather than figuring out what is causing it in the first place, then you set yourself up for repeated and more serious injuries. Solving the root issue will not only solve the immediate problem but can—and should—help you adjust your training going forward. Perhaps you are overdoing it in one area, lack strength in a part of your body, or need to be doing more in the way of preventive measures.

Treatment

Once you have found the root of your injury, you need to plan your next move. The problem may be something you can treat yourself, or you may need to turn to an expert for examination and diagnosis. It is easy to assume that simply taking time off is an answer to most running-related maladies. Yes, days off can help in a lot of instances, but using that as a default approach is not always wise. You might only be delaying the diagnosis of your actual problem or extending the length and severity of your injury.

Once you've gotten a proper diagnosis of your ailment, then you can take steps to heal it and move past it. Below are some basic treatments for the most common running ailments, some of which involve measures you can do yourself and some of which require an outside expert. Treatment varies depending on the scope and severity of the injury.

- *Tendinitis:* anti-inflammatory measures—rest, ice, ultrasound, and anti-inflammatory medication.
- *Muscle strains or tears:* rest, ice, ultrasound stimulation therapy, and light massage once the injury begins to heal.
- *IT band syndrome:* ice; ultrasound stimulation therapy; sports massage; pelvic realignment; loosening of the quad muscles, piriformis muscle, and iliotibial band.

- ***Plantar fasciitis:*** rolling and loosening of the arch; calf stretching; arch support; night splints; avoidance of barefoot walking, sandals, or flip-flops; ultrasound stimulation therapy.
- ***Achilles tendinitis:*** calf stretching, calf massage, light Achilles massage, and anti-inflammatory medication.
- ***Hamstring or abductor pain:*** rest, ice, pelvic realignment, massage.

Bringing in an Expert

Sometimes preventive measures are just not enough, and our bodies break down. As part of your responsiveness, finding the source, and treatment, you may need outside assistance. Working with someone you trust and who has worked with and had success with other athletes is very important.

Massage

Sports massage is an effective way of promoting muscle health as well as part of an effective treatment for some muscle tears, IT band syndrome, and other strains. I'm not referring to a spa massage focused on relaxation and rejuvenation. A sports massage might have aspects that are relaxing, but its objective is to get the muscle to the healthiest state possible. Like the foam roller, a massage can do wonders for blood flow, removal of toxins, alignment of muscle fibers, and specific tight spots. Identifying and relieving a specific tight spot, especially one not right at the surface, is difficult to do with a roller, stick, or other self-massage tool, but a good therapist will be able to work out knots, kinks, and sore spots in muscle groups or segments very effectively. A good sports massage also helps with overall recovery.

A good sports message therapist will understand that thoroughly working a muscle is beneficial but that going too deep can create other problems. Tell your therapist the amount of pressure you'd prefer and ensure that he or she understands that your goal is to rejuvenate muscles, not add intensity that only creates more stress or discomfort. In an attempt to loosen a particular muscle, some massage therapists wind up inflicting more damage to areas that were not suffering previously. I had a few such massages myself and ended up feeling that the massage created a new issue that I had to deal with instead of achieving the end goal of promoting comprehensive muscle health.

A good therapist has a moderate touch and a discernment of how much is enough and what areas need more attention than others. As mentioned earlier, you still want some functional tightness, or "pop," in a lot of your leg muscles (especially in the hamstrings), so avoid having a therapist work too much on one area, which can overloosen a muscle. I once worked with a therapist who worked my hamstrings so much that they felt loose and unresponsive for several weeks. They lost the functional tightness that builds the necessary tension to create more power. In that situation, my hamstrings felt dead and unresponsive from too much deep-tissue work in one specific area.

The proper sports massage lets you target specific areas but is general enough to hit a wide range of muscle groups as needed. It should have solid pressure, and it might be very uncomfortable at times (especially when the therapist is working on soft tissue that is overly tight), but it should not leave you sweating and squirming on the table due to the pain you are undergoing at the hands of your therapist.

A good massage once a week would be an incredible treat to your muscles, but that might not be an option you can afford. I received massage work about every 7 to 10 days, but only during the bulk of my hardest training. During my Base Phase, I extended that out to every two to three weeks because my training was volume-based but not very intense.

Addressing Alignment

Along with stretching, foam rolling, use of a massage stick, or sports massage, the other element of overall structural balance is proper alignment. By "alignment," I refer primarily to pelvic, sacral, and lower-lumber positioning and configuration. Of course, spinal alignment is also part of the equation, but I focus on those particular areas in regard to preventing the most common running injuries.

Attention to alignment has become much more prevalent in recent years, but many runners still have no concept of how their pelvis is affected by and correlated with the motion of running. There has been much discussion about core strength in the past decade, and core strength is important because it has a direct correlation with proper pelvic alignment. With good core strength comes a more likely propensity to stay in correct alignment, but a weak core or an imbalance in core strength allows the pelvis to shift more easily. Once the pelvis and sacrum are out of alignment, they require manipulation to get back. Like cogs and gears of an engine, they are meant to fit together in a certain way so that the mechanics of running can be smooth, efficient, and as effective as possible. Once out of whack, these areas need to be manually put back in place and maintained, with a greater emphasis on certain exercises until balance is regained. Having well-rounded core strength built from a regular routine ensures that things will not shift around as easily.

My IT band injury during my freshman year of college exposed me to the importance of alignment. As I mentioned earlier, I missed competing during the first semester due to the issue plaguing one knee; then, during the second semester, it shifted to the other knee. My lack at the time of consistent stretching and core strength routines, as well as my being continually dehydrated, all contributed to the IT band becoming excessively tight and thus pulling on the attachment at the side of my knee. My muscles were so unaccustomed to consistent maintenance that it took several months for them to respond to massage and stretching. Everything was so gummed up that it took a long time to release the tension.

Aside from adding consistent stretching and massage during the second semester, I also began to focus on core strength and alignment. At the time, I was a very skinny runner who lacked natural core strength. In the early 1990s, no one was really talking about core strength or crosstraining as a means of injury prevention for runners. Sit-ups and other old-school fitness exercises had come and gone out of fashion, and there was no real focus on other ancillary components of training. It was all about running.

I started seeing a chiropractor at the advice of one of our assistant coaches. For the first time in my athletic life, I became aware that my pelvis and back affected my legs and their functional movement patterns. Up until that point in my running career, I did not know that my pelvis could even get out of alignment, much less that it would cause a running injury.

But when you are injured and cannot run, you think about it a lot, and if you're smart, you learn as much as you can about what caused a particular injury and how to proactively prevent others from occurring. My treatment up to then had been about 75 percent accurate in that I took care of the muscle responsiveness, started thinking about hydration, and treated the inflation at the knee, but until that point I was not treating the true source, namely, pelvic misalignment. My structural misalignment was causing an elongation of the IT band and thus causing it to pull on the attachment. Sure, my muscles were very tight, and it took more time than it should have to release the tension, but even when my muscles were once again responding correctly, I could not get the knee pain to subside. My pelvis was not aligned correctly, and therefore the IT band was still not functioning properly. The chiropractor got my pelvis realigned, and I was back to running in a few weeks.

Once I was back in alignment, everything else followed suit. With continued core work, I was able to able to keep my hips aligned properly and return to running pain-free. This experience opened my mind to how critical pelvic alignment is to the functionality of the muscle groups associated with running. But it also showed me that it wasn't just one thing that was causing my lateral knee ailment, nor was there a simple one-step solution for it.

After college, I integrated structural alignment via a physical therapist on a regular basis. I was training at such a level that I required either weekly or biweekly adjustments. Essentially, my muscles and core were being taxed so greatly that I could not maintain proper alignment and thus needed consistent help. (This was only during the bulk of my hardest training during the year, not necessarily during my off-season or Base Phase.)

My therapist had an extremely good touch and ability to identify subtle issues. Often little adjustments made a big difference in my gait fluidity and thus improved my training and efficiency immensely. This level of ongoing adjustment is not necessary for most people, but it is important to note that proper alignment is crucial for all runners.

As I got further along in my career, I could tell quickly when my hips needed adjustment. I could also tell when my upper back needed attention or my ribs or psoas needed work. The more attention I paid to these matters, the better I got at recognizing an issue early. By listening to your body, you start to recognize early on when something feels a little bit off and, hopefully, can stop an injury in its tracks.

Structural alignment is often neglected in a runner's injury-prevention routine, but it is extremely important. Many people have some type of underlying alignment issues that don't surface until they start training harder or reach their late 30s. Maintaining proper alignment should be included in your overall approach to injury prevention, and if the regular help of a physical therapist or chiropractor is not a viable option for you, then it should at least be one of your first steps when an injury does surface. Dealing with one particular injury after college started with a visit to my physical therapist. We started with the pelvis and lower-lumber region and worked from there to determine the problem. A good physical therapist (or sports chiropractor) will be able to address your alignment and also look at other treatments for all muscle groups, joints, attachments, and related ailments.

Choosing the Right Expert

No matter whether you have big or small ailments, align yourself with professionals whom you trust who can diagnose your situation properly and assess your next steps with the notion of what they mean for your running. My first line of defense was always my physical therapist, followed by a very good massage therapist. Those two in combination fended off almost every issue I faced along the way.

A physical therapist or a reputable chiropractor with a focus on athletes is a great first stop. They can work on structural issues as well as some soft-tissue problems that are trickier to understand. A good therapist will be able to diagnose whether a muscle is firing properly, whether it is a tendon-related injury based on stress tests of the area, or whether it is something else entirely. He or she will be able to provide a treatment plan in most cases. If the issue is related to a bone or some type of tendon rupture, then seeing a doctor—such as a podiatrist or an orthopedic specialist—is the next step. Many people jump to this step and skip the physical therapist or sports-focused chiropractor. The problem with this approach is that most specialists don't have ongoing experience with soft-tissue issues. Their first thought tends to be a surgical approach, and they may not consider all of the other options before going that route. However, if there is any suspicion of a stress reaction or stress fracture, then seeing a specialist is very appropriate.

Running Shoes 101

Running shoes are the only vital piece of equipment you need for running, and it is important to find the right ones for you. From overbuilt stability shoes to minimalist models to ultracushioned shoes, runners have more options than ever. There's been an amazing evolution in running shoes in recent years, but you have to be mindful of what kind of runner you are and the kind of shoe you need and not just be interested in trying the next best thing.

Are you a new runner? Have you been running for 10 years? Have you been running in the same shoe for 15 years? Have you become stale wearing a certain shoe or type of shoe? Are you injury prone? Those are the questions to ask yourself before you choose a shoe.

The single biggest variable in choosing your shoes is a good fit. A "good fit" means that a shoe conforms to and accommodates both the size and shape of your foot. Every manufacturer builds shoes on different three-dimensional lasts, which means every shoe will fit the shape of your foot a little bit differently.

Try the shoe on, and consider things such as toe-box height and width (your toes should not touch the front or top of the shoe), how the laces hit the top of your foot, whether the shoe holds your heel in place without having to over-tighten the laces, how the shoe snugs down your arch and creates a cohesive connection between your foot, the shoe, and the ground. Can you feel the ground through the shoe and derive proprioceptive awareness that allows you to run with good, uninhibited form?

continued >

My advice for committed enthusiast runners is to rotate through one or two pairs of daily trainers and a pair of lightweight trainers. This will allow your feet to recover (or avoid being burdened by the same foot-strike patterns every single day) and will help each pair last longer and feel better every day.

The daily trainer, which has a little more cushion and support, should serve as the primary shoe for your long and easy runs, and sometimes even tempo runs. Lightweight trainers, which are more agile and have slightly less cushioning and considerably less structure, are best for harder and faster workouts two to three times per week. Lightweight trainers work well for tempo runs, fartlek workouts, occasional long runs that have a progressive pace, and interval sessions on the track. They should also be your first choice on race day, as they promote a more efficient foot-strike pattern based on shoe geometry. They can give your body a different stimulus and also help enhance the workouts and the racing experience.

Start by visiting a running specialty shop and try on several styles of daily trainers and lightweight trainers. Jog around the store before you consider buying anything. Step-in comfort is great, but you need to find out how the shoes feel when they are laced up and how your foot moves in them while running. You will quickly know if you are trying out the wrong shoe, and you should also be able to sense which shoes feel right.

Be choosy about the person whom you are entrusting with any major health decision. That person should have your best interest in mind and needs to consider your running as part of the process. A second opinion is often appropriate. I always went back to my trusted physical therapist with any outside diagnosis. If a specialist felt I needed an invasive approach, I would take that question back to my most trusted resource.

In 2003, a toe injury came on quickly. I had run a solid 27:41 in a 10,000-meter race on the track on a Friday night at Stanford University in Palo Alto, California, and by the following Tuesday, I knew something was off. The joint was painful and swollen. My physical therapist suggested I get it scanned and analyzed by a foot specialist based on what his own tests indicated. This injury came during a heavy track-specific training period during which I was doing multiple hard track sessions each week while wearing track spikes. Coupled with high weekly mileage and some questionable training shoes I was trying at the time, I had put my foot in a vulnerable position.

The specialist ordered an X-ray, which indicated that I had a partial tear of the plantar plate in my second toe. Basically, the sheath around my second toe joint that keeps all the fluid encapsulated was damaged. Dye was injected into the joint to test whether the joint capsule was compromised. If dye leaked out, then the capsule was ruptured. This test was pretty definitive, and so was the specialist's intent to fix the issue. What is not definite is the recovery from such an injury, especially for an athlete.

The specialist insisted that my season was over and that I needed surgery to fix the tear. Recovery from the surgery was six months. He said that if I continued to run, my toe tendon could rupture completely. He showed me alarming pictures of toe tendons that had ruptured and basically scared me into thinking that surgery was my only option. Looking back, I am shocked at his eagerness to so quickly perform surgery on me. At the time, I was the top 10,000-meter runner in the United States, just a few weeks away from the national championships. It takes a massive amount of either arrogance or ignorance to nonchalantly suggest surgery with a six-month recovery for anyone, much less someone who makes his livelihood from running.

I considered the assessment and stewed over it for several days while trying to get the symptom to calm down with ice and anti-inflammatory medications. I did not get a second opinion, but I did trust my instincts. I had run through a lot of issues and had become very good at listening to my body and knowing how it reacts. As I was contemplating my next step, I visited a man who makes custom inserts and is adept at creating unique inserts with a specific purpose. He made a custom piece for me that had a cutout for that toe joint. Basically, it allowed the swollen and damaged toe joint a void so that the joints on either side would bear the weight. I tried the insert and ran without aggravating the situation. I kept running, and although I was not entirely pain-free, I could tell I was not doing more damage. As long as I supported the other joints around the injured toe and did not put pressure on it, then I could run and even do hard workouts on the track. He made me a second pair of ultralight inserts that I could fit into my track spikes.

The moral of the story? I listened to my instincts and took a calculated risk. Two weeks after that specialist's bold statement that I needed surgery with a six-month recovery, I placed second in the Bolder Boulder 10K road race with no ill effects. Two weeks later I ran 27:55 to win another 10,000-meter race on the track at Stanford, beating a loaded field that included Meb Keflezighi. I continued running for the rest of that summer and placed 14th in the IAAF World Championships in Paris. After the track season, I took a few weeks off, and the toe healed and never bothered me again.

Diagnosis and treatment of injuries are not always cut-and-dried. Be careful whom you listen to, and be sure the assessment or treatment matches what you are feeling. Sometimes an aggressive approach is appropriate, but not always. Be creative. There may be a smart way to continue to work toward your goals even if you have an injury to contend with.

– 9 –

RACING

My first exposure to competitive running came when I was in fourth grade. It was a simple mile run in gym class, but it forever changed my life. We did not run the mile on a track or around soccer fields but rather around a field that was several inches deep with gravel in some spots. El Paso, Texas, didn't have nice groomed fields, and the elementary school did not have a track. Picture running through sand, and you get the idea what we were up against. No matter—I never thought twice about the surface. For me, it was all about the competition with my classmates and ultimately the clock. I was excited to race, even though I had no idea how to pace myself or how far a mile really was. Eager, excited, and very green, I seized the moment and took it to my classmates that day, winning the mile in 6:27 and showing for the first time in my life that I might have some talent as a long-distance runner.

After that, I do remember a sixth grader named Carlos Cacharna, who had recorded the fastest time in the school with a 6:05, stopping me in the hall to ask what my time had been. Being the fastest kid in the school was a badge of honor, something that gave you immediate bragging rights. Carlos wasn't keen about me encroaching on his territory, and I remember looking up at him and, with a slight hesitation, telling him my time. He smirked and said, "Not bad."

I was excited that running had brought me a little notoriety among the older kids in school. But that wasn't what inspired me to keep running. What inspired me to stick with running was how amazing I felt while racing. Although I was only minimally trained and really just running from my natural talent, I enjoyed the feeling of running confident and free and strong. I did not fully comprehend it at the time, but being able to combine physical, mental, and emotional energy to run fast in a race was a huge thrill that brought with it a totally satisfying sense of accomplishment. Two years later, as a sixth grader, I broke the school record with a 5:44 mile. This was the spark that ignited my passion to pursue competitive running. Racing to my max felt fantastic.

Let's face it: Daily running may be our stalwart, constant companion, but racing is where the excitement lies. But although racing can be fun and exhilarating, it isn't easy, and it shouldn't feel that way. You'll likely feel both good and bad and everywhere in between during a race. While training is about hard work and structured efforts, different variables come into play during a race. There is more pressure surrounding a competition—inherent pressure based on our own goals and expectations as well as from outside influences such as coaches, parents, or teammates—than there ever would be in a workout. And that makes racing much more than a physical endeavor. Having a clear mind and a sharp focus to support the physical demands of a race are crucial to success. To race to the level of your fitness demands that you find a happy medium among your physical, mental, and emotional energies both before and during the race. There are numerous ways to wrangle mental strength and emotional energy to help the process.

Earlier in this book we explored what kind of runner you want to be, what motivates you, and your commitment to doing what it takes to become the best runner you can be. Those elements are not only key aspects to your goal-setting, training, and daily routine but are also instrumental catalysts for your race-day execution. The principles you followed in training are more than just motivational tools; they are the lynchpins to race success.

Even with those things firmly in mind, be aware that successful racing also takes time and experience. Learning how to compete and how to get the most out of yourself has a trial-and-error aspect. As a teenager, I was a very good runner and ran fast times compared with those in my age group, but it took a while for me to learn the nuances of racing. I was fortunate to have a supportive coach and parents to help guide me through my development, but ultimately I had to learn how to race on my own. All runners must go through the process on their own in order to figure out what they need to do.

The beauty of running a race is that it is a solitary act that forces us to face our fears and challenge ourselves.

The beauty of running a race is that it is a solitary act, one that forces us to face our fears, be accountable to ourselves, and challenge ourselves. While others certainly play a role in your progression as a runner, only you can take the reins and make it happen during a race. No matter what your running experience is, you need to be ready and willing to push yourself—by yourself—to your physical, mental, and emotional limits in order to chase your goals.

Although races occur infrequently and happen quickly, they should be approached as a process, just as training is, with the principles discussed early in this book diligently applied. Races are special moments when opportunity meets execution and we have a chance to push ourselves beyond our previous boundaries. Assuming your training is complete, the best way to ensure optimal racing results—executing a maximal effort on race day, or what I call "racing to your fitness"—is to build a smart race-day strategy.

Developing a Race Plan

Imagine traveling to Europe without making any advance arrangements. It might feel exciting, but it certainly wouldn't feel comforting. While your trip might be exhilarating at times, it would inevitably include some aspects that did not go well, such as getting lost, taking the wrong train, or ending up at a dumpy hotel. You would probably spend much of your time figuring out your next step instead of taking in all the amazing things around you, seeing the sights, or visiting a museum. When you run a race, you want all the aspects to go well. Like a great trip to Europe, it takes intentional planning ahead of time—not on-the-fly decision making—in order to ensure a successful experience.

In 2002, at the age of 30, I tested my fortunes in the marathon for the first time. I chose the Chicago Marathon. Up to that point in my career, I had proven I could win national titles in shorter distances on track and in cross country, run sub–4 minutes for the mile, qualify for U.S. national teams, and compete with some of the best runners in the world. But I was not as competitive on a world level as I wanted to be. Even with a personal best of 27:33 in the 10,000-meter run, I was never in position to win a medal in a major championship. I had qualified for four IAAF World Championships and competed in the 2000 Olympics in that event yet was still not able to achieve the highest level of success. Although I had earned the chance to represent the United States in those events, I hadn't yet been as competitive as I thought I could be.

To shift successfully to the marathon, I knew I needed a well-thought-out training strategy and a race-day plan. Generally speaking, while the distance was different, I was able to apply the same fundamental principles to my training that had helped me achieve success earlier in my career at shorter distances. However, mileage became my biggest focus. While training for a marathon is not simply a function of increasing mileage, mileage certainly is a bigger factor than it is for 5K and 10K training. I prepared diligently with a buildup that included running at least 120 miles a week for eight weeks and a peak of 135 miles a week for a few weeks. I also made a concerted effort to maintain my speed, as I knew that was one of my assets.

Going into that marathon, I was healthy, fit, and confident, which helped me to feel focused and calm. I also had what I thought was a good race-day plan that allowed me to be prepared for the physical act of running 26.2 miles and getting to the starting line healthy and motivated. My one flaw (as I described in the previous chapter) was that I didn't account for running in much cooler weather. Although I had a successful race, I ultimately could probably have run much faster if I had adjusted my fueling plan to match the lower-than-expected temperatures. The combination of those things contributed greatly to my sixth place, 2:09:41 finish, which at the time tied me with Alberto Salazar for the fastest debut marathon in U.S. history.

Having a plan was key to my finding that winning balance of focused yet relaxed. I struggle with being too focused and holding on too tightly to a desire to perform well. Having a specific plan, and knowing I had stuck to it and trained diligently, gave me the confidence I needed to relax and focus on race-day execution. Just as a pre-race routine creates order for race weekend, so does having a race-day plan create order for your race. And with order comes confidence and comfort.

A good race plan should take into account your goals—both your time goal (for example, 2:45 or 3:00 or 3:15) and anything else you hope to achieve from the race (for example, finishing in the top 10 percent, running well in your age group, or running negative splits). But it should also include an honest review of your training. Reflecting back on your training can offer cues as you fine-tune your race plan. If everything went as planned during training and your buildup races showed good progress, you might be in position to run faster than you expected when you started your training program, perhaps even finish with a PR. If so, develop a race plan that puts you in position to go for it in the second half of the race.

Or perhaps you are confident in your aerobic fitness heading into a race but less so in your speed because of missed or ineffective workouts. If you were injured or missed training because of work, travel, or family obligations, you might be fit but not as fit as you expected to be. If that's your reality, the best thing you can do is prepare to adjust before and during the race. In particular, be careful about going out too fast and risking completely blowing up. The best way to monitor your race is to check your splits every mile as well as at intermediary points (5K, 10K, etc.) and gauge how you feel. If you feel great at the 10K mark of a half-marathon or marathon, keep running strong, holding back just a touch so you can also run strong in the final miles. Conversely, if you feel like you're running beyond your limits at the 5K mark, it might be time to back off a bit.

Once you have a good gauge of your fitness going into the race, consider other variables such as the weather conditions and specific aspects of the course and how those will affect your race strategy, your nutrition plan, and your adaptation during the race. For example, if it's going to be warmer than normal, decide how and when you'll consume more liquid and calories during the race. If you know it's going to be windy at a certain point in the course, consider adjusting your pace expectations for the times when you're running into the wind or running with the wind at your back.

Know ahead of time where mile markers and other key points of the course are located. If your race has a long downhill section at the start (for example, the Boston Marathon), an uphill section at the start (for example, the Marine Corps Marathon), a rolling profile (for example, the New York City Marathon), or relatively big hills in the middle (for example, Boston, the Twin Cities Marathon, or the San Francisco Marathon), figure out how those features mesh with your race strategy, pacing, and goals. For example, if your goal is to break the 3-hour barrier in the marathon, you'll have to average about 6:52 per mile, but be aware of places on the course where you might run slower or faster based on the terrain. If you expect your halfway split of the race to be exactly half of your time goal, but course conditions dictate a slightly slower or slightly faster half, don't let this come as a surprise. It's one thing to say you want to run a negative split over the second half of your race, but it's another thing to actually execute it. Plan ahead, and have a good idea of what your splits will realistically be based on all of the variables.

The bottom line is that nothing should be a surprise, even if the weather changes drastically. Building a race-day plan based on your training, fitness, and goals will help you prepare for whatever comes your way and give you the best chance at achieving—or surpassing—your goals.

Build Flexibility into Your Plan

Just because you have a plan does not mean you won't have to deviate from it, but better to have a plan and then change it during the race than to have no plan at all. If you are running solely on chance and emotions, then you are bound to make a mistake or react too swiftly to things that happen in the early part of a race. The longer the race, the more exacerbated those mistakes become. In a shorter race, you can get away with your pacing being slightly off or your hydration not being completely dialed in, but in a longer event, everything is magnified. Stand at the end of a marathon and watch athletes finish, and you will get a sense of this magnification; it is not pretty.

Too, while a race may be yours alone, you do not race alone. I recall discussions with Meb as we ran through the olive groves in Crete in the weeks leading up to the Olympic Marathon. He would diligently go through various scenarios to ensure that he was clear on what he might possibly expect. This included not just his own execution plan but also scenarios his competitors might employ. This was where I struggled in my race-day planning. I was very good at analyzing my fitness, my pacing calculations, and my specific plan based on my goals. However, I typically failed to think through what my competitors might do and how I would react. Meb, on the other hand, talked as much about the competition as he did the course, the hills, the weather, and other details. That kind of strategic focus helped him develop into a world-class marathon champion and become the only runner ever to win an Olympic medal and both the Boston and New York City marathons.

You may not be looking to win a race, but you still need to consider how those around you will affect your race. As you think about your own individual race, be sure you put it in the context of the larger event and the group around you, whether it be the anticipated pace of the starting wave you're in, the pace group you signed up for, your training partners, another runner who starts out really fast, or a joker intent on racing you up a midrace hill. Think ahead of time about how you will react to those situations.

Visualize Your Race

No runner should arrive at the starting line of a race without having first visualized how that race will go. Thinking through the race in acute detail—from the moments before you approach the starting line to the moment you cross the finish line—will give you the best chance of performing optimally and making adjustments on the fly.

Visualizing your race—seeing yourself hitting your pace and reaching your goal result at the finish line—is a key mental step to keep you focused and relaxed. It's best to do this a few times in the weeks leading up to your race but especially important in the days before your race as you make final preparations. It's also a good time to consider adjustments that might be necessary based on weather or how you feel.

Start by imagining how it will feel to approach the starting line. You might sense some pre-race nervousness; that's good. Picture yourself in race-day gear, the exact clothes and shoes you'll be wearing, and see your race number affixed to your singlet or shorts. Go through the motions of the moments just before the starting gun goes off and think about how you will start the race according to your race strategy.

Next, picture yourself in the first third of the race. Can you imagine what the pace will feel like? Can you picture yourself getting into a rhythm and pace that are in accordance with your planned strategy and time goal? You will probably feel anxiety or eagerness; that's normal. During this visualization, you'll want to remind yourself to trust your training. This helps you keep a calm mind, knowing you have put in months of training to prepare physically and mentally for the excitement and discomfort that start to settle in as the race draws near.

It is possible that early excitement or the fast pace of others around you might cause you to go out too fast. In your visualization exercise, think about how you will react if you come through the 1-mile mark or the 5K mark too soon. Can you visualize how you will tell yourself to relax and get into a rhythm that is in line with your race strategy and goal time? Conversely, if you come through the initial splits too slowly, you'll have to adjust your cadence and pace to be more aggressive. You don't want to panic and surge too quickly, but instead adjust your pace and methodically get that time back gradually. Thinking about these situations and responses prior to the race will better prepare you to make key subtle adjustments before it is too late.

Think too about how you'll feel midway through the race as fatigue and discomfort set in. How do you want to react? Think in advance about how you will stay positive and mentally and emotionally calm as your body goes through the physical rigors of running at a fast pace. Do you have a mantra you can repeat to keep yourself on track?

Finally, think about how you will feel during the final part of your race. You're not only going to have to deal with feeling physically strained, but you're going to have to keep negative thoughts at bay. Reminding yourself to expect discomfort should be enough to keep you on the razor's edge of preparedness once you get to race day.

Be Focused, Yet Relaxed

Focus is essential to racing well and being ready when it counts, but so too is relaxation. Holding on too tightly or caring too much makes it difficult to keep it together when a race starts to hurt or be challenging. It takes a concerted effort to relax, enjoy the process, and execute.

It took years for me to learn how to find the balance of being focused yet relaxed. I had the focus part down but needed to work on relaxing. Along with my Chicago race, I remember an instance when successfully mastering that balance was key to a great race. I was working toward a personal best in the mile, with a race coming up in which to test myself. I had also qualified to run the 5,000 at the 1998 Goodwill Games in New York. There was no IAAF World Championships that summer, so I just raced domestically and in Europe. But my summer of racing hadn't been going well, which was getting stressful. I ran a lackluster 5,000 on a Thursday at the Goodwill Games, flew home on Friday, and then flew back to St. Louis on Saturday to compete on Sunday in a tribute meet in Illinois, where I would test my mile. Flying back and forth across the country and running a 5K three days prior was not what I considered a proper buildup to a personal best.

What did I do? I made a conscious decision to let it go. When I stopped holding on so tightly, although still focused, I finally relaxed. On Sunday, I ran a new personal best of 3:55.1 for the mile and beat a majority of the field, including several world-class mile specialists. Talk about satisfying! Sometimes you race well when you least expect it, and often the key for me was learning to relax.

Some athletes are the opposite, craving more intensity and stimulation in order to focus. They have to be in the action, at the track and shakeout the day before the meet when all their competitors are there, hobnobbing with athletes, agents, and coaches. However, those types are relatively rare. Most athletes need to relax in order to perform well, not get more pumped up before the race.

Preparing to "Go for It"

We don't get many chances to do something special, something that will continue to be meaningful years afterward. Defining moments like that in running are not just about winning. No matter what kind of runner you are, whether you're a high school runner racing the state championships, trying to reach a Boston Marathon qualifying time, or completing your first half-marathon, if the goal is important to you, it's worth laying it on the line and just going for it. It comes down to staying strong when the going gets tough and never settling for less than your best effort. While it is easy to let yourself off the hook in the heat of the moment, what you really need to do in that moment is to go for it.

"Going for it" does not necessarily mean pushing harder or going out faster or doing something drastic. Often it is the opposite. It requires patience, having a calm mind, assessing the situation, making a conscious decision. It does, however, require you to move out of your comfort zone mentally and emotionally. Doing something exceptional, specifically running to your fitness in a race, requires an ability to manage discomfort. This is one reason that we train. We put ourselves through ongoing discomfort in training so that on race day we are used to this sensation. The hope is that you have prepared your mind as well.

As mentioned in Chapter 3, "Creating Balance," I am an advocate of building up all your emotional energy and focusing it on the event. Being ready when it counts and poised to go for it requires you to come to race day fresh and energized. If you have trained properly, you have put yourself in enough uncomfortable scenarios to be ready to manage the physical discomfort and mental exercise of a race. What comes next is translating all that work, both mental and physical, into an effective performance.

Racing is full of difficult moments that require you to push yourself amid increasing fatigue, acute discomfort, and mental anguish. Racing is not just a physical pursuit but also one that involves mental strength and emotional calmness. Therefore, in order to go for it in a race and lay it all on the line, you must create an environment for success both physically and emotionally. Balance is as important on race weekend as it is in training.

To make matters trickier, no two race situations are the same. How you feel on a given day, how your body responds, and how a particular race unfolds are unique to each race experience. There are, however, some best practices to follow that will increase your chances of achieving success, such as wielding your emotions to your advantage, building a smart pre-race routine, and minimizing distractions.

Controlling and Unleashing Your Emotions

For the majority of my racing experiences, I ran to the level of my fitness thanks to a successful collaborative effort between physical preparedness and mental acuteness. My best performances occurred when I found the correct balance of the proper fitness, a mental focus on execution, and an emotional detachment about the desired results. If you focus too much on the results before or during a race, you won't stay in the moment mentally in order to execute an effective race. If you let your emotions take over, you are likely to mentally fold, which can lead to a physical collapse as well.

During my professional career, I followed a mantra before and often during a race that kept my priorities straight: Stay focused yet relaxed, mentally acute yet emotionally detached. In the last 15 percent of a race, let your emotions help carry you in. It was simple and to the point, but it affirmed my intent and helped me maintain control of a racing situation.

In the spring of my senior year in college, I was entered in a 5,000-meter race at the Mt. SAC Relays in Riverside, California. Up to that point, I had had a lackluster season. I had trained hard but had yet to see the fruits of that effort due to an Achilles injury and some periods of inconsistent training. It was a stressful situation made even more emotional because I knew that my college career was winding down, and I wanted to prove myself at this level. The race had a competitive field with many runners who were faster than I, but fortunately, conditions were ideal for distance running on the track—temperatures in the mid-50s, low humidity, and no wind.

Because we didn't really know what kind of shape I was in, Coach Wetmore and I didn't have a clear race plan. We had decided to just go with the pace of the group and see how it played out. But moments before I stepped out onto the track, Mark told me to "shoot for 13:45 pace, and just go out in the back one-third of the pace for the first lap." I was taken aback because we had spoken about breaking 13:40 earlier in the week. However, the second part of his advice was calming because he knew the leaders would go out hard and run the first lap in 60 seconds, which we both knew was too fast. His last-minute advice allowed me to very deliberately start the race emotionally detached.

That is not to say that I did not care about how I was racing or wasn't invested in the outcome. Much the opposite, actually. Instead of reacting emotionally to the fast start of the leaders, I was able to focus on running my race. I started out toward the back of the field of 20 or so runners, still coming through the first lap in 63 seconds—however, I felt controlled and comfortable. With no expectation and no sense of pace after the first lap, I was running hard but without emotion, letting my physical self take over and run lap after lap with just enough mental acuity to run smart. I found myself slowly moving up. Before I knew it, there were four laps remaining, and I was in 10th place. During the final mile, I began to sense that I was having a special race. Suddenly feeling strong and confident, I allowed myself to get emotionally involved and started to surge past as many people as possible over the final 600 meters. The final laps were a blur, but when it was all over, I finished third in the race in a new personal best of 13:31.7 and later learned that I had run a 4:06 last mile.

In any race, try to remain emotionally detached—most of the way. It is a tricky skill to execute because of all of the preparation and sacrifice you've put in, but remember, it does not mean you don't care. It just means you will focus on the physical act of running during the beginning and middle stages of a race. Then, during the final 15 percent, you can let your emotions fuel you. In the case of my 5,000 race in Riverside, being emotionally charged helped me run a strong final 800. For a marathon, the final 15 percent of the race is roughly the final 4 miles. You might find yourself emotionally engaged sooner or later than that, but the key to running to your fitness and achieving optimal race results is spending most of a race driven by a rational brain, saving your emotionally charged passion for the final portion when fatigue and discomfort are at their highest levels. At that point, it's time to throw rational thinking out the window, dig deep, and just go for it.

That was exactly what I was able to do in the 2005 Boston Marathon. I came into the event very fit and with a newfound confidence in the marathon distance, having run 2:09:41 in my first race in Chicago in 2002, won the 2004 U.S. Olympic Trials in record time on a cold day in Birmingham, Alabama, and then taken 12th place in the Olympics. I knew I could run at a world-class level in the marathon, and Boston was the perfect stage.

The first half of the race was about execution, and I simply ran with the lead pack. We were running conservatively in 85-degree, windy conditions. But as the pace started to get faster after mile 15, runners began employing different tactics. Soon the pack had broken up, and the race was on. I decided to stick to my plan and stay mentally focused on execution, not allowing myself to react emotionally about starting to lose contact with the front-runners. This calm execution carried me through the Newton Hills, and by mile 19, I was starting to pass some of the casualties who had reacted too soon, hadn't had the fitness to surge so early, or were suffering from an ineffective nutrition plan on a warm day.

By the time I crested the final hill and made my way past Boston College, I was in 10th place. My legs were feeling the effects of 21 miles and warm conditions, and I knew it was time to let my emotional engagement take over. We all have moments in a marathon when we have to make a decision. I decided I was not going to let myself off the hook, not settle for running OK or putting out a 90 percent effort.

Emotionally energized and feeling good despite the fatigue and discomfort, I passed a few more runners between miles 22 and 24 on Beacon Street. As I made the final turn off Hereford Street and onto Boylston Street, almost at mile 26, I passed Robert Kipkoech Cheruiyot, the Kenyan runner who would win the Boston Marathon the following year and several other major marathons after that. His surprised look at me said, "Who is that guy?" I finished fourth, the highest finish by an American in 17 years at the time. It took everything I had in the last 15 percent of that race, but it was well worth the effort, and I was glad that I had stored up as much emotional energy as possible during my training and during race weekend so that I was able to unleash it when I needed it.

I wasn't able dig to this level in every race, and as I progressed in my career, I found it harder and harder to go to that place. This was a reason why I raced sparingly—I knew my emotional limitations. But the thrill of it all coming together in that moment when you need it most is unparalleled.

The Importance of Pre-race Routines

An effective pre-race routine can help you handle the mental burden and intensity that often accompany an important race. Having a routine helps you keep emotions in check and creates a sense of control.

With any important event, something you have trained for and dedicated yourself to, there is that inevitable out-of-control feeling that accompanies the situation, and it is magnified the closer the event gets. The more important something is to you, the more out of control you can feel. This is why I was brought to tears on several occasions, including the afternoon before the Olympic Trials in 2000 and the night before the event in 2004. It felt so out of my hands, so out of control, that it literally brought me to my knees.

The closer you get to the race, the less you should think about your emotional engagement with it. Visualizations as race day nears should be emotionally detached and matter-of-fact. While on race day it's OK to shift back to some level of emotional investment, keep your thoughts on less-draining imagery in the days leading up to the race. It is difficult not to think about your goals and how important they are to you. Simply saying to yourself, "Don't think about the race," will not work. You must provide some other form of focus. A pre-race routine focused on such matters as your nutrition and hydration plan, pre-race meal planning, packet pickup, travel arrangements, and adjustments for weather conditions will help you keep your emotions in check in the days leading up to an event.

Your pre-race routine should be flexible enough to be adjusted based on travel hiccups or other unforeseen problems. But just as with your race-day hydration and nutrition plan, you want a pre-race routine that you can count on, plan for, and then alter as needed. Having an effective pre-race ritual also creates a predictable set of circumstances that you can duplicate before each race to ensure that you are physically and mentally ready on race day.

Containing Your Energy

A pre-race routine also helps control the release of energy. For months, you've been storing physical, mental, and emotional energy as you trained and planned for your race. Now, as if you've stored it in a gallon-sized jar, you want to be able to open that jar and release it all on race day.

Be careful not to let it escape in the days before a race. For some, this happens at the expo; for others, it is a function of too much chat in the lobby or before the race while hanging around to warm up. Other people get pulled into emotional-energy drains by engaging with other runners' nervous banter. It can start with a friendly "Are you here for the race?" but then progress to a dialogue related to your training, injury issues, or how you felt on your morning shakeout run. This is not the time to discuss such matters. Smile and keep it simple, and keep all of that energy for yourself. Picture yourself walking around with that gallon-sized jar full of energy that you've built up through months of training and planning, and don't let the energy escape.

Take particular caution with energy when traveling to a race. For many runners, the excitement of being in a new city in the days before a race causes them to lose track of important details or expend excess energy walking around the race expo or sightseeing. Enjoy yourself, but remain focused, and be conscious of what you do. Spend some time at the race expo, but don't make it a half-day activity. Pack your race-day kit and any necessary nutritional supplements so that you don't need to spend time shopping or browsing for hours. Mind your fueling and rehydrating strategy from the moment you arrive. Runners who travel to an out-of-town race often end up going from the airport (when they're dehydrated from the flight) to the expo (without having eaten a proper meal) to their hotel (even more dehydrated) to immediately doing a short shakeout run to loosen their legs before eating a late dinner. This is a good example of what not to do.

Now, as if you've stored emotional energy in a gallon-sized jar, you want to open that jar and release it all on race day.

Plan your meals—what, when, and where—so you don't get caught eating food you're not comfortable with or get stuck waiting in line at a restaurant. As discussed in Chapter 7, "Diet, Fuel & Hydration," make sure you're not going long periods between meals or eating excessively large meals, as both can become hugely detrimental come race day. Instead, think about continually refueling and rehydrating from the moment you arrive in town. Eat small healthy snacks on a regular basis—fruit, granola bars, or energy gels—to top off your glycogen stores and avoid hunger pangs. Carry a water bottle so that you can continually rehydrate in the days before the race.

A pre-race routine is essential not only to help provide mental focus but to ensure that your body feels as good as possible and that you can run to the level of your fitness. If you are racing locally, you still need a routine and plan.

The day before your race, make sure you have your race-day kit laid out in your hotel room ready to go. Include everything—shoes, socks, clothing, and a "throw-away" shirt that you can ditch at the start line if running a road race on a cool morning—and pin your race-number bib to your shirt. Know exactly where and when you need to be at the starting line (or on a bus that will take you to the starting line), and, especially if it's cold, plan on a time to jog a mile or two to warm up.

Being intently focused on race details doesn't mean you can't relax a bit, but save sightseeing, shopping, and shows for after your race. Make sure you do an easy shakeout run each day you're in town before a race, especially after you get off an airplane. If you're too relaxed, then the inevitable strain that accompanies a significant race effort comes as a shock mentally and physically. Again, you have to find that balance of focus and relaxation so that your mind and body stay acutely engaged with the reason you're really there.

Dealing with Distraction: Two Olympic Tales

2000 Sydney Olympics: Too Many Distractions

I earned a spot on the 2000 U.S. Olympic team by finishing second behind Meb Keflezighi in the 10,000-meter run at the U.S. Olympic Trials in Sacramento. I was thrilled to make my first Olympic team and excited to take in all that was associated with the experience. That process started the very next day, when we got fitted for Olympic uniforms. We tried on all the various outfits, from the opening-ceremony uniform to the race-day kit to what to wear if you win a medal. To go through that experience the day after making the team was thrilling. I was 27 years old and remembered that day 12 years earlier when I had written down that I wanted to qualify for the Olympics. It had taken almost half my life to realize that goal, and I planned to enjoy every moment of it. I certainly wanted to run well in the Olympics, but in hindsight, it is clear that my focus was more on just being happy to be there. Plus, I was unprepared to deal with the distractions and hoopla.

From the start, the one damper on the lead-up to the Olympics was that Shayne had finished fourth in the trials in the 1,500-meter run, one spot and 2 seconds from earning her own Olympic berth. Because Regina Jacobs had qualified in both the 1,500 and the 5,000, all Shayne could do was hope that Regina would choose to focus only on the 5,000 and give up her spot in the 1,500. Shayne was an Olympic alternate, so the USOC paid for her flight and allowed her to participate in the U.S. training camp in Brisbane the week before the Games started. Amid all of the excitement of being there, we did our traditional training with track workouts and then had an opportunity to explore some of the countryside. We ran on the outskirts of town and saw wild kangaroos bound across the dirt road in front of us. We also had a private tour and show at the Brisbane Zoo with the late Steve Irwin. It was an amazing time, full of once-in-a-lifetime experiences.

On the fifth day of our training camp, Shayne got the news that Regina was out of the Olympics, and that changed everything. This was the love of my life, my best friend, so of course it affected me directly. Between the trials and the moment when she found out she was on the team, I was disappointed, elated, stressed, and relieved right along with her. This unique situation led both Shayne and me to just be content to enjoy ourselves and take in all the Olympics had to offer. As events unfolded, my focus shifted from racing to simply enjoying this incredible experience alongside my wife. We went to opening ceremonies, watched other sports such as gymnastics and swimming, and went sightseeing in Sydney. To this day, the only framed picture we have in our home from the Olympics is one of the two of us walking into the Olympic Stadium together. I would never have been the athlete I was, never have developed into the person I was, and certainly not have made that team without her as my partner. Truth be told, I was really just glad to be there; racing was an afterthought, and that felt OK.

But by the end of the third week and with all we had gone through, I was physically and emotionally spent. I was unfocused and too relaxed. This coupled with being halfway around the world and surrounded by 5,000 other athletes put me in a vulnerable position: I got sick. Four days before I was set to compete in the preliminary race of the 10,000-meter run, I was in bed with a fever and congestion. I tried to stay positive and set my focus on racing, but the cards were stacked against me at that point. I ran the race, finishing last in the second heat in 29:00.71. With all that we had gone through to get there, to wind up sick really put a

Race-Weekend Questions

Here are questions to ask yourself as you create a pre-race routine for an out-of-town race:

- *What time does my flight land, and in what time zone?*
- *When I land, how long will it have been since I had a good meal?*
- *How convenient is it to get to the expo?*
- *What do I need to do at the race expo?*
- *How long will it take to get to the hotel?*
- *When and where should I do a short shakeout run?*
- *When and where should I eat dinner?*

damper on the experience. Although I had not expected to win, I was most disappointed by not being able to give my best effort. Still, I would not have changed how sweet it was to experience all that Shayne and I did together. And, even better and much to my surprise, not being able to run to my potential set me up to perform better than I ever have over the next four years. I would get a second chance at my Olympic dream.

2004 Olympics: Putting It All Together

My 2004 Olympic experience was entirely different. Not only had I won the 2004 U.S. Olympic Trials Marathon, but Shayne had also earned another Olympic berth. Four years after the disappointment of finishing fourth in the 1,500-meter run in Sacramento—and giving birth to our first son in the interim—she returned to the same track in Sacramento, California, with the same pressure and won the 5,000-meter run with a sprint finish at the line.

My focus on racing was much better, partly because I was better prepared to handle the distractions and events leading up to my race. We traveled to Greece to the U.S. training camp on the island of Crete. We stayed at Pilot Beach Resort, which was relaxing, quiet, and calm. We decided to bring our 2-year-old son with us because we knew we would run better if he was there, but Shayne's sister was there to help take care of him.

It was comforting to be around the rest of the U.S. distance runners, especially Meb Keflezighi. He and I did the majority of our running together, and this proved highly beneficial to my marathon performance. Talking about the course and how we would deal with the hot conditions, not to mention hearing Meb's unwavering determination to earn a medal, helped keep me calm and focused. Although I was struggling to regain all of my fitness after an injury I had suffered earlier in the summer, running on the lonely dirt roads of Crete with Meb and other teammates helped rebuild my confidence in my running.

I wound up running 100 miles in the week before my race. That wasn't my normal practice, but it turned out to be exactly what I needed. Perhaps more importantly, because I was running so much, I had a sharp mental focus on the race and on how my body was reacting to the hot, humid conditions. And unlike the experience in Sydney, this time Shayne and I did not go to the opening ceremonies, did not watch other sports, and did not go sightseeing. I was there to race, and the last week in Crete was spent in solitude.

I spent four nights in Athens before the race, but I was determined to spend as little time as possible in the Olympic Village because of my fear of getting sick, as I had in Sydney. I spent one loud, restless night there but transferred to a makeshift dorm room at a local college campus that the USOC used as its headquarters during the games. Because there were no other sleeping accommodations on campus, a few classrooms had been turned into bedrooms. I ate in the small cafeteria with the USOC staff, relaxed in my classroom, and did my final shakeout runs before my race. Shayne had finished competing and was staying in a hotel with our son and my parents. She would have preferred to stay with me, but they would not allow the family to join me at that point.

Race day was hot—a sizzling 82 degrees at the 6 p.m. start. I lost contact with the front group after a big downhill at mile 9 and eventually fell back to 25th place. But I remained calm and emotionally detached, trusted my fitness, and moved up gradually over the next 12 miles. I moved up to 10th place by mile 21, only to struggle on the final downhill section and get passed by several runners. I kept fighting and stayed focused, then let my emotions kick in to carry me home. I entered the stadium in 15th place, pushed hard on the lap around the track, passing three more competitors, and finished 12th.

My 2004 Olympic marathon performance is one of the most satisfying performances of my career, not because of where I placed but because I finished knowing, without a doubt, that I had run to my potential. On that day under those conditions, given the circumstances of my buildup and with all that goes into any marathon, much less one six time zones away, I was thrilled with the effort. After all of the post-race meetings, interviews, and mandatory drug testing, I finally got back to my dorm room at about 2 a.m. I showered and looked in the mirror and was both reminded of how much better this experience was than my experience in Sydney and thankful that I had not returned to my makeshift hotel disappointed.

Racing is a fine balance of art and science. Finding that precise equilibrium between being calm, relaxed, engaged, and focused is different for everyone. Meb did not stay isolated in a classroom for the three days leading up to the race, yet he performed to his ability on that day. I knew what I needed to stay mentally acute and emotionally detached, all the while being relaxed, and it worked out perfectly for me. Racing well takes a conscious awareness of how you are wired, a keen observance of what has worked (or not worked) in the past, and intentionally and proactively creating an environment that allows you to be successful.

AFTERWORD

There is both a science and an art to training for performance-oriented running goals. The science is based on the physiology of the human body: understanding how it applies to your own physiology and following time-tested training principles in order to continually progress. The art is about being true to who you are based on what motivates you, what frustrates you, how running fits into your life, and how your life fits into running. That part comes down to being honest with yourself, understanding how you're wired, and removing limits and barriers in order to create a holistic approach to your running.

As this book illustrates, achieving a high level of performance requires an ongoing systematic approach that demands your attention and dedication. Understanding what drives you, adopting psychological strategies, creating a feasible life balance, following a training plan that caters to your personal abilities and goals, and being proactive about nutrition and injury prevention are all specific elements that must be integrated in order to reach your personal running goals.

Following the principles and practices outlined in this book, I was relentless in my pursuit of excellence at every level of my running—from the time I started as an adolescent through my high school and college careers and for 12 years as a professional runner. Now, as a coach, I offer those same principles to runners of all abilities and try to help them reach their goals. These principles are universal and supersede the trends and fads related to training, racing, gear, diet, fuel, hydration, and other aspects of running and fitness that come and go from time to time.

Many of you may already be doing some of the things I've outlined in this book, but more than likely there are some holes to fill to create a truly comprehensive approach. Virtually every runner—from one just starting out to elite competitors—can examine his or her own training and find places to apply many of these practices and principles. Some of you might have major gaps to fill, while others may need only to slightly tweak a few aspects of their approach to lead the next level.

I'll be the first to admit that I made a lot of mistakes along the way; the experience I share in this book was hard-won. But my running was always a work in progress, an evolution of continually building on what I had learned or experienced in previous seasons. The further I progressed, the smaller the changes that I made—but each one was still significant when factored in to the collective. Although I was self-coached for most of my professional career, I wasn't simply making it up as I went along, doing whatever I felt like on a given day. I was using these principles and practices, along with knowledge and experience gained from across my entire career, as part of a systematic approach to continue my development.

My goal in writing this book was to capture a collection of principles, practices, and information from which any runner can benefit and to illuminate those things that helped me continually improve and perform at a high level as a runner through sharing my own experiences.

Ultimately, when you get to the starting line of a race, you want to feel confident, physically prepared, and emotionally energized, knowing you did everything you could to get there. It's not easy to do. Your development as a runner will take time, hard work, and relentless dedication. There will be high points and low points, and there are no quick fixes or magic-bullet workouts. But with a commitment to these principles and time-tested practices, I believe you can—and will—achieve all the success you desire as a runner.

INDEX

fast running and fast racing, 134

fast-twitch muscle fiber, 110, 134, 137–139

fatigue: anaerobic training for, 105; anticipating and planning for, 100, 217, 220, 222–223; in Base Phase, 108; helped by grazing, 152; injuries from, 196–197; with lactic acid buildup, 130, 136–137, 143; maintaining form, 187–188; from overtraining, 91–93; response time for, 195

financial incentives, 30

fitness assessment tests, 144

fitness levels, beginning, 102, 105–107

fitness levels, gauging, 214

flow, 52–56

foam rollers/massage sticks, 192

focus and relaxation, 218–219

Foot Locker shoe stores, 31

footwear. *See* shoes

forward arm circles with skip, 187

Found, Shawn, 62, 65–66

fueling. *See* diet/fuel

functional muscle tightness, 180, 200

gait analysis, 161

gastric-emptying rates, 162–163

Gatorade Sports Science Institute (GSSI), 161–163

generic approaches, 87–88

glutes stretch, 182

glycogen regulation, 128, 152–153, 170, 226

goal setting, 16–19, 26–28, 30–35, 36–38, 213

going for it, 219–220

Goodwill Games, 1998 (New York), 218

Goucher, Adam, 62, 79, 81–82

GPS-integrated tracking devices, 88, 92–94

grapevines, 188–189

grazing, 152–153, 173–174, 226

group training, 53, 61–64, 85, 87–88

half-marathon training: buildup races, 113–114; glycogen depletion, 170; lactate threshold training, 104; long intervals, 131; long runs, 135; tempo runs, 135, 140

Hall, Ryan, 159

Hallman, Hugh, 74–75

hamstring extensions, 189

hamstring pain, 199

hamstring stretch, 181–182

hard vs. intense effort, 77

Hauser, Brad, 7

Hawpe, Brad, 57–59

heart rate: heart rate monitors, 144; heart rate training, 92–93; hydration effects, 168; tempo/aerobic threshold runs, 140; during workouts, 144, 168–169

Henderson, Joe, 122, 126

high altitude running, 124

high knees, 190

high school running career, 31–35

hill workouts, 136, 139–140

holding back, 85–87

holistic injury prevention, 176

hydration: daily plan, 165–166; dehydration effects, 71, 168; fueling with, 156–161; heart rate and, 93; as injury prevention, 183–184; muscle function, effects on, 168–170; optimization, 168–169; oxygen, effects on, 168–169; perspiration and, 163–164; pre-race hydration, 226; on race days, 156–161, 170–171; science of, 161–163; during training, 170

IAAF (International Association of Athletic Federations), 2, 89, 208

ice, running on, 66

iliotibial (IT) band syndrome, 24–25, 138, 175, 193, 195–198

illness, 47, 69–70, 107

incentives, psychology of, 29–30

injuries, 175–208; alignment, 201–204; cooldown routine, 186, 190–192; daily routine, 178; distance running injury rates, 176; dynamic drills, 187–190; expert help, 199, 204, 206–208; foam rollers/massage sticks, 192; hill workouts, 139; hydration, 183–184; jogging, 185; massage, 199–200; pain vs. discomfort, 193–194; pre- and post-run routines, 181–182; proactive injury prevention, 177–178; response time, 194–196; shoes, 205–206; sitting stretches, 182; sources of, 196–198; with speed work, 138; standing stretches, 181–182; stretching, 179–183; strides (buildups), 186; treatment, 198–199; warm-up routine, 184–186. *See also* illness

instincts, trusting, 45–47

intense vs. hard effort, 77

International Association of Athletic Federations (IAAF), 2

ABOUT THE AUTHORS

Alan Culpepper grew up in El Paso, Texas, where he held five state championship titles in track and cross country; he still holds numerous El Paso city records some 25 years later. While studying at the University of Colorado–Boulder, he was an eight-time Division I All-American and earned a national title in the 5,000 meters at the 1996 NCAA Championships held in Eugene, Oregon. Alan graduated in 1996 with degrees in sociology and geography and was named the University of Colorado's student-athlete of the year. In 2012, he was inducted into the University of Colorado Athletic Hall of Fame.

Over the course of his 12-year professional career, Alan proved to be one of the most consistent and versatile distance runners in American history. His success culminated with qualifying to represent the United States in the 2000 and 2004 Olympic Games. In the 2000 Sydney Games, he competed in the 10,000 meters, and in 2004 in Athens, he ran the marathon. In addition to his two Olympic showings, Alan was a seven-time U.S. national champion with two titles in cross country, five in track, and one in the marathon. He qualified to compete on four World Track & Field Championships teams as well as numerous World Cross Country Championships teams. In 2002, Alan ran his debut marathon in a time of 2:09:41,which at that time was the American debut record and placed him sixth in the Chicago Marathon. In only his second marathon, Alan won the 2004 Olympic Marathon Trials and later that year went on to an impressive 12th place finish in the marathon at the Athens Olympic Games.

He continued a string of impressive performances, finishing fourth in the 2005 and fifth in the 2006 Boston Marathon. With a range of personal bests from 3:55.1 in the mile to 2:09:41 in the marathon, Alan has the best range of any American distance runner to date.

Alan lives in Boulder, Colorado, with his wife, Shayne (who is also a 2000 and 2004 Olympian), and their four boys.

Notable Accomplishments

Olympic Team Member, 2004 and 2000

4th place, 2005 Boston Marathon

5th place, 2006 Boston Marathon

12th place, 2004 Olympic Marathon, Athens, Greece

Olympic Trials Marathon Champion, 2004

Marathon American debut record, 2002, 2:09:41

World Championships team member, 2003, 2001, 1999, 1997

12K Cross Country U.S. national champion, 2007, 2003, 1999

10K U.S. national champion, 2003, 1999

5K U.S. national champion, 2002

8-time Division I NCAA All-American

5K Division I NCAA national champion, 1996

Personal record mile: 3:55.1

Personal record 5K: 13:25.6

Personal record 10K: 27:33.9

Personal record marathon: 2:09:41

Brian Metzler is the editor in chief of *Competitor Running* magazine and Competitor.com. He has run more than 60,000 miles in his life, tested more than 1,200 pairs of running shoes, raced every distance from 50 yards to 100 miles, and completed two Ironman triathlons. He was the founding editor and associate publisher of *Trail Runner* and *Adventure Sports* magazines and formerly a senior editor at *Running Times.* He has written about endurance sports for *Outside, Runner's World, Triathlete, Inside Triathlon, Men's Health,* and *Men's Journal* and is the author of *Running Colorado's Front Range* and coauthor of *Natural Running.*